INDIA AND CENTRAL ASIA

INDIA AND CENTRAL ASIA

PRABODH CHANDRA BAGCHI

GYAN

Published by

Gyan Publishing House
5, Ansari Road
Daryaganj, New Delhi-110002
Phone: 011-47034999, 9811692060
E-mail: books@gyanbooks.com

Distribution Network
gyanbooks.com
India, USA, Canada, UK, Australia

ISBN: 978-93-7133-473-0 (PB)
First Published, 1955

2nd Impression 2025

Printed at: Gyan Press, Delhi.

INDIA AND CENTRAL ASIA
Author Prabodh Chandra bagchi

INDIA AND CENTRAL ASIA

PRABODH CHANDRA BAGCHI

NATIONAL COUNCIL OF EDUCATION, BENGAL

INDIA AND CENTRAL ASIA

BY

PRABODH CHANDRA BAGCHI,

HEM CHANDRA BASU MALLIK
Professor of Indian History
(1949-1951)

NATIONAL COUNCIL OF EDUCATION, BENGAL
CALCUTTA 32
1955

CONTENTS

PREFACE

The present book is substantially the lectures delivered by me at the National Council of Education, Bengal, during 1949-1951 as the Hemchandra Basu Mallik Professor of Indian History. It has been my endeavour to give here an outline history of the ancient cultural relations between India and Central Asia. Many of the problems are complex and their final solutions are yet to be found. However a considerable amount of specialised studies on various aspects of the problems has accumulated. I have not felt competent to use all their implications in the presentation of my subject. Besides personal worries have also interfered with the best I could do. In the Appendix I have reproduced three of my old articles of a technical nature bearing upon some of the problems ;—of these : *The Role of Central Asian Nomads in Indian History* was my presidential address to the Indian History Congress held at Aligarh and published in Greater India Society Journal 1943 ; *Culika Śulika and Culikā Paiśācī* was published in the Journal of Letters, Calcutta University, 1931 and *Kuchean and Western Arśi* in Indian Historical Quarterly 1934.

I am grateful to the National Council of Education for the opportunity they gave me to prepare these studies. I offer my sincere thanks to the Registrar, Sri P. C. V. Mallik for the interest he has taken in the publication of this book. I also thank my pupil Sri Subhamay Ghosh for helping me in the preparation of the Index.

I regret that due to lack of facilities proper diacritical signs could not be used in the earlier part of the book.

Santiniketan
10th October, 1955

P. C. BAGCHI

CONTEMPORARY PERIODS OF CHINESE HISTORY

Former Han 206. B. C.—24 A. D.
Latter Han 25-220
Shu Han 221-264
Wei 220-265
Wu 220-280
Western Tsin 265-316
Eastern Tsin 317-420
Former Leang 317-376
Former Ts'in 350-394
Latter Ts'in 384-417
Western Ts'in 385-431
Northern Leang 386-439

North :

Wei Toba 381-534
Wei, Western 535-557
Wei, Eastern 534-550
Ts'i 550-557
Chou 557-581

South :

Song 450-478
Ts'i 479-501
Leang 502-556
Ch'en 557-589

United Empires :

Sui 589-618
T'ang 618-907
Song 960-1279
Yuan (Mongol) 1280-1368

INDIA AND CENTRAL ASIA

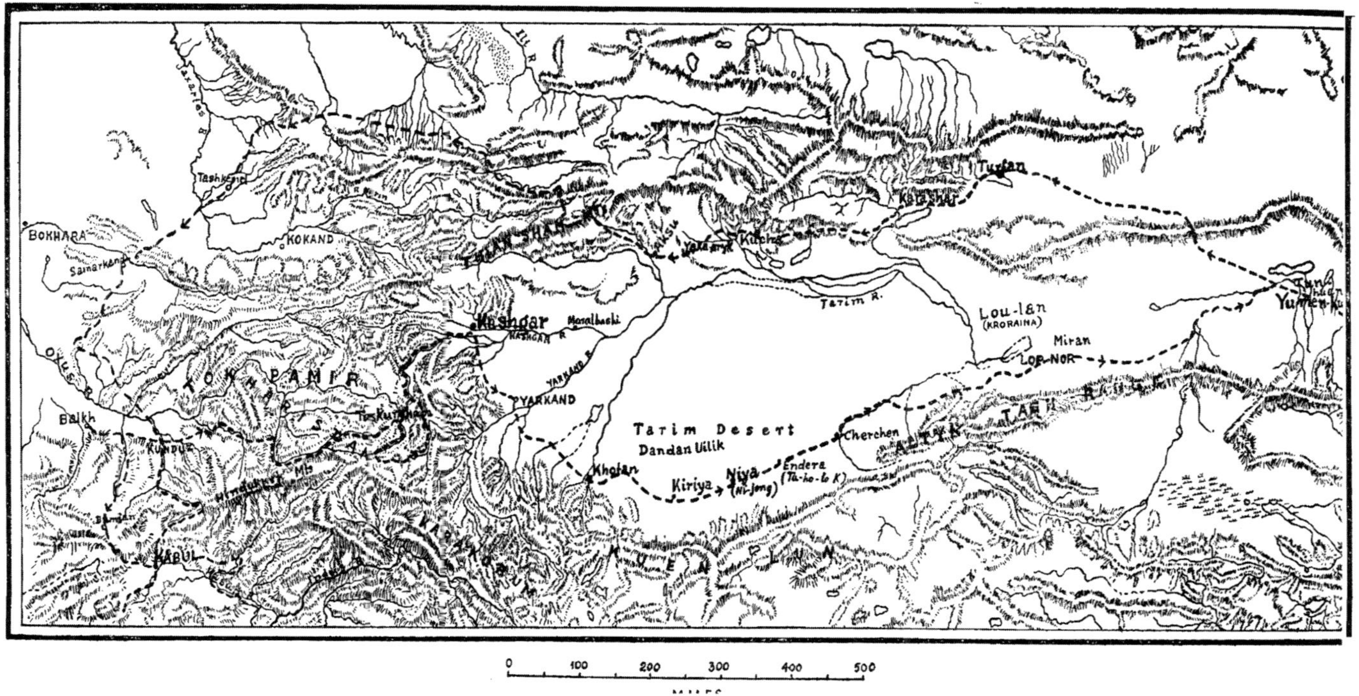

INDIA AND CENTRAL ASIA

CHAPTER I

NOMADIC MOVEMENTS IN CENTRAL ASIA

SCYTHIANS

With the dawn of history we find Central Asia divided into two zones, one nomadic and the other sedentary. The northern steppes from South Russia to Manchuria constituted the nomadic zone, whereas the region to the south including the oases of Eastern Turkestan was the zone occupied by sedentary people. The nomadic zone again seems to have consisted of two distinct regions : that from South Russia up to the valley of Ienessi was occupied by nomadic hordes of Aryan stock known as Scythians and that in the east, including Outer and Inner Mongolia, Manchuria and further east, was occupied by Turco-Mongol hordes. In the south, the land between the Jaxartes and the Oxus was occupied by settled people of Iranian origin. What is later known as Eastern Turkestan, a territory from the Pamir region up to the frontier of China, was also occupied by Aryan-speaking people of different affiliations. The movements of the nomads of the steppes either on the west or on the east affected the sedentary life in the south through centuries, and brought about far-reaching changes in the political history, not only of Central Asia but also of the Persian and Chinese empires and of India.

The earliest information on the Scythian nomads is available from the account of Herodotus and the old Achamenian inscriptions. The Scythians are generally mentioned as Skuthoi by the Greek writers, and as Ashkuzai by the Assyrians. They were known in Persia as Saka and in India as Śaka. Under the name 'Scythian' were included various tribes of Indo-European origin, who spoke either Iranian or other Indo-European dialects. They were the nomadic sections of the Iranians and other Aryans left behind in the northern steppes who had refused to adopt the culture of their sedentary congeneries in the South.

The old Persian inscriptions speak of three different tribes of these Scythians who were living in the North in the region extending from South Russia up to the Central Asiatic steppes. They were : (i) Saka Haumavarka, who are more literally the Sakas of the Persian and Indian literature, settled in the region of Ferganah and extending up to Kashgar. (ii) Saka Tigrakhauda or Sakas with 'pointed caps' who spread towards the Aral and occupied the lower valley of Jaxartes. (iii) Saka Taradraya, or Scythians who lived beyond the seas in South Russia. Other allied races were the Sarmatians, Massagetes, Arimaspes, Issedones etc. mentioned by Herodotus. The Sarmates were probably neighbours of the Scythians of South Russia. As the name indicates, Massagetes (Massyagata — "fisherman") spoke an Iranian language, and lived near the Aral. The Issedones and the Arimaspes lived to the east in the northern steppes, the former in the region of Irtych and Ienissei. As the name Arimaspes is Iranian, meaning 'lover of horses,' (ariamaspes) there is no doubt that they were Scythians. The Issedones are regarded by some to have been of a different race, probably Finno-Ugrian.

The Scythians, like the Iranians, had a social organisation consisting of three classes — warriors, priests and agriculturists. They had not, however, accepted the Zoroastrian religion. Their religion seems to have been of the primitive Indo-European type. They worshipped, as Herodotus tells us, such Gods as Vesta, Jupiter, Apollo, Venus-Urania, Hercules, Mars and Neptune. He does not give the Scythian names of these gods excepting for some. Vesta was called Tabiti, Apollo — Oetosyrus, Venus-Urania — Artimpasa and Neptune — Thamimasadas. Jupiter was considered by the Scythians to be Papaues, father, and Earth, — Apia or mother. This conforms to the Vedic conception according to which Dyaus is *pitar* and Prithivi is *matar*, and the two are juxtaposed as Dyava-prithivi. Vesta may be compared to a Vedic deity like Vastospati — the deity of the hearth and home ; the Scythic name of Apollo clearly connects him with sun-god, — *Syrus* is Surya and *Oeto* may be connected with Vata. The Scythians, like ancient Aryans, were not used to erect images, altars and temples, and their mode of worship was to offer sacrifice to the gods. They had numerous soothsayers or shamans who divined with the help of a number of willow rods by placing them on the ground and uttering predictions. Such practices were known also among the Vedic Aryans.

The relics of ancient Scythian art and weapons show that they lived in a bronze age which continued in certain areas till the 2nd century A. D. The easternmost centre of this culture was in Siberia in the upper valley of the Ienessei near about Minussink. It was a metallurgical centre which produced knives, daggers, cup-like cauldrons in bronze from the 5th century B. C. to about the 3rd century A. D. These are relics of a Scytho-Sarmatian culture which are to be found all over, from Inner Mongolia in the east to Hungary in the west.

Although there had been earlier movements of the Scythian hordes from the Central Asian steppes to the West, the sedentary civilisation of China, Central Asia, Persia and India do not seem to have been affected much by such movements before the 3rd century B. C. Since then the movements became continuous till the times of the great Mongol invasions, and affected the civilisation of almost the whole of sedentary Asia. Most of these race movements started from the Mongolian deserts, and set in motion all the nomadic tribes in the west.

HUNS

The earliest of these movements to be started from Mongolia was by a people called Hiung-nu in ancient Chinese history. The Hiung-nu, in spite of certain uncertainties about the ancient form of their name, were, for all practical purposes, the same as the Unnoi and Hunni respectively of the Greek and Latin writers and the Huna of Indian literature. They were known to the Chinese long before the 3rd century B. C. while living in the north of China. About the middle of the 3rd century B. C. they became united and strong under a chief who had the title Shan-yu. The headquarters of the Chief was in Mongolia near Qaraqorum. From various indications in the Chinese history about their language and customs, it appears that they were Turks and not Mongols. Once united, they started their campaigns against China, and China also, united under the great Ts'in Emperors, took various measures to check their depredations. The Great Wall was built to stop their inroads from the north, and in 210 B. C. they were completely ousted from the region of Inner Mongolia.

The Huns now tried to enter China from the west by way of Kansu, which was not protected either by natural barriers or walls. Western Kansu was occupied by a people mentioned as Yue-che in the Chinese Annals. The Huns now fell upon the Yue-ches in 176 B. C., completely defeated them, killed their king and drove them out of Kansu. The Yue-ches were scattered; the greater bulk of them migrated to the west, whereas others moved to the south, to the Nanshan region.

The destruction of the Yue-ches of Kansu made the Huns more powerful, and they started afresh their depredations in Chinese territory. China was, however, fortunate in having a powerful Emperor in the person of Wu-ti of the Han dynasty, who was on the throne from 140 to 87 B. C., and a number of great military leaders. The Huns were incessantly pursued on all fronts and defeated everywhere. The great Chinese general, Ho-kiu-ping, drove them out of Kansu. Two Hun tribes—Huen-Sien and Hiu-ch'u—submitted to the Chinese and accepted their vassalage (121 B. C.). Western Kansu was reorganised into four military districts—Leang-chou, Kan-chou, Su-chou and Lan-chou. In 108 B. C., the Chinese army pushed further westwards and established their authority in Lobnor and Turfan regions. Here again the Chinese came into conflict with the Huns. The latter, having been driven from Kansu, tried to control the northern part of the Tarim basin. In 77 B. C. the King of the state of Loulan near Lobnor was punished for joining the Huns and a military garrison was established there. In 71 B. C. the Chinese army proceeded up to the Ili region to help the nomadic people called Wu-sun, established there, against the Huns. In 67 B. C. the State of Kiu-she (Turfan) was conquered for allying itself with the Huns, and in 65 B. C. Yarkand was compelled to accept Chinese suzerainty. In 60 B. C. a Chinese military garrison with a Governor-General was established near Karasahr.

Soon after, a civil war between two rival claimants for chieftainship divided the Huns. One of them named Hu-han-ye became the Chief in 33 B. C. with Chinese backing. The other claimant, Che-che, then moved west and defeated other nomadic people in Russian Turkestan — the Wusun in the Ili region, Hukie of Imil, and K'ien-k'u of the Aral region, and settled in the Talas region. The Chinese army, however, followed them there, and inflicted a crushing defeat on them in 36 B. C. and killed their chief. The remnants of the horde went over to Europe and were heard of much later in the 4th century A. D. under Attila.

The Hun empire of Mongolia was destroyed in 155 A. D. by a Mongol horde called Sien-pi (Sirbi). The Sien-pi chief, in his drive against the Huns, advanced up to the Ili and inflicted a defeat on the Wusuns. The Sien-pi empire, which was a short-lived one, extended from Manchuria up to the Balkhash. The Sien-pi, after their victory over the Huns, turned against the Chinese, conquered Inner Mongolia in 156 A.D. and invaded Kansu. About the beginning of the third century they were thrown back, and the Hun tribes were re-established in Inner Mongolia to guard the frontiers.

YUE-CHES AND PEOPLE OF THE TARIM BASIN

The Hun incursions into Western China were the cause of the dispersal of some of the sedentary people of Central Asia. Before the Huns came down, the position of the tribes was somewhat as follows: After the destruction of the Persian empire by Alexander, a Greek kingdom had been founded in Bactria which comprised practically the whole area from the north of the Hindukush to the Oxus and probably portions of Chorasmia in the north-west. The Greek domination in Transoxiana, if any, was temporary and of an uncertain character. Transoxiana was occupied by the Sogdians (known as Sughdik or Sulik), an Iranian people with their distinctive civilisation. Their northern neighbours were the Sakas, another Iranian people with their distinctive language.

The position of the tribes in the Tarim basin i. e. Chinese Turkestan can be gatherd to some extent from ancient Chinese records and Central Asiatic archaeology. The northern part of the

Tarim basin, Kucha, Karasahr, up to Western Kansu was occupied by an Aryan people allied to the Yue-ches. They were probably a branch of the ancient Scythians speaking, not an Iranian language, but an independent Indo-European dialect of which the remnants are now found in what is called ancient Tokharian. The Greek writers, Strabo, for example, in the 1st century B. C. speak of them as Tokharoi. The Sogdian tradition mentions four tribes of the Tokharian people (Toughri) in the northern part of Chinese Turkestan, Beshbaliq, Karasahr, and Turfan. Ptolemy in his geography places a people called Thaguroi, a mountain called Thaguron and a city called Thogara in the region of Kansu. We may therefore consider, for all practical purposes, the people called by the Chinese, Yue-che, as identical with Tokharoi, Tukhara of Indian literature.

A people allied to the Yue-che, the Wu-sun of Chinese accounts, another Scythic tribe, was settled in the valley of the Ili river in the region of the lake Balkash. Some scholars would identify them with the Asiani of the Greek writers, but the old Chinese pronunciation of the name would point out to something like (G)usun or (G)usur. In all appearance, the oases to the immediate north and south of the T'ienshan up to the western part of Kansu were occupied by the Indo-European speaking Yue-che or Tukhara people at the time when the Huns came down from the North. They had spread in the distant past from the west to the east and might have been a branch of the people vaguely described by Herodotus as Scythians. The people which lived in Kucha, Karasahr, Turfan and surrounding areas down to the time of the Uigur invasion in the 8th century, and ultimately merged into the Turkish people, were branches of the ancient Yue-che or Tukhara people.

The southern oases of Eastern Turkestan, Kashgar, Yarkand, Khotan, Niya, Lou-lan (Lobnor region) up to Tunhuang were also occupied by other Indo-European peoples whose identities cannot be clearly established. From later evidences it appears that they were branches of the Saka people living in Transoxiana, speaking an Eastern Iranian dialect. Their appearance in that region in the 2nd century B. C. is testified by Chinese evidence.

Presence of Indo-Aryan speaking people cannot also be ruled out in the southern oases right up to the frontier of China. Herodotus (III, 98ff) seems to speak of all this area as a part of India. He says that part of India towards the rising sun is all sand, and that the country towards the east is a desert by reason of the sand. The desert people, according to him, were nomads, ate raw flesh and had Scythian customs in regard to the disposal of their old men and women. India proper is distinguished by Herodotus as the country lying towards the south of Persia, bordering on Caspatyros (Kashmir), and Pactyica (Pakhta). The inhabitants, according to him, resembled the Bactrians and were never subject to Darius.

It is, therefore, clear that long before the 2nd century B. C. when the Huns appeared on the western side of China and ousted the Yue-ches from their possessions, Indo-European speaking people occupied the entire central belt of Central Asia including the area now called Chinese Turkestan right up to the frontier of China. A considerable part of the province of Kansu up to Leang-chou was also an Aryan territory, being included in the possessions of the Yue-ches.

The Kukunor area, to the south of the Yue-che territory, now called the Chinghai province of China, was occupied by a very powerful people of nomadic habits called K'iang by the Chinese. These K'iangs are usually supposed to be the ancestors of the Tibetans, but from accounts given in Chinese Annals it seems likely that they had also certain affinities with the Aryan nomads perhaps on account of the contiguity of their homeland with the Yue-che territory. From about the 4th century B. C. till the 2nd, China had been constantly menaced by K'iang incursions deep into the Chinese territory from the West.

When the Yue-ches were defeated by the Huns in 176 B. C. and compelled to leave their own territories in Kansu, they were divided into two sections — the Siao Yue-che (Small Yue-che) and Ta Yue-che (Great Yue-che), so called probably on account of their numerical strength. The former moved to the south of the K'iang country and mixed with them, but the latter, the Great Yue-che, moved towards the west on a more important migration which affected the political history of the countries to the west considerably. The Great Yue-ches, instead of following the route towards the Tarim basin, followed the north-western route along the foot of the Altai towards the Ili region to the territory of the Wu-sun. The Wu-suns were defeated and allowed their victors to live in their territory for some time, but later revolted against them and drove them away with the help of the Huns.

The Yue-ches, after being ousted from the Ili region by the Wu-suns, moved further westward and came to the country which the Chinese called Ta-yuan and which corresponds to the region of Fergana. Tashkend, Ferganah and Kashgar were then occupied by the Sakas, the Saka Haumavarka of the early Achamenian inscriptions, Sakai of the Greeks and the Śaka of Indian literature. The Yue-ches occupied Transoxiana and forced the Sakas out of the country. The Sakas first occupied Sogdiana and then moved further south and destroyed the Greek kingdom of Bactriana— mentioned in the Chinese accounts as Ta-hia, corresponding to Tokharestan. The Yue-ches, however, pursued the Sakas to Bactriana, and under their pressure the latter migrated to North-Western India.

The Yue-ches were ousted from Kansu in 176 B. C., occupied Transoxiana about 160 B. C. and established themselves in the Oxus valley soon after. It is well-known that they founded a powerful empire in this region and the Chinese Imperial envoy came to them in 128 B. C. to seek their help against the Huns. We know that the Yue-che, instead of getting involved in war with the Huns, slowly consolidated their power in the Oxus valley, later conquered Kabul and North-West India and founded a mighty empire under the rulers of the Kushan dynasty, which lasted till about the 3rd century A. D. Even after the fall of this empire their branches continued to rule parts of India and Bactriana till the 5th century A. D. Yue-che emperors of India are known in history as Kushans, but in Indian literature as Tukhara. Thus the nomadic movement of the Huns which started in Mongolia in the 3rd century B. C. set other tribes and nations in movement and their waves reached ultimately the civilised areas of Iran.

HEPHTHALITE HUNS

In the beginning of the 5th century A. D. we hear of another race movement in the Central Asian steppes, which again had its effect on the political history of India and Iran. A Turco-Mongol race, usually known as the White Huns, more correctly called Hephthalites, who originally lived in the Altai region, started extending their dominion westward. The Persian historians mention them as Hayathelite and the Chinese say that they took their name from Ye-t'a or Hephtha, which was the name of their ruling clan. In fact these are the people who are known in Indian texts as Huna.

In the beginning of the 5th century they were not an important people and owed allegiance to another nomadic tribe of Turkish origin called Juan-Juans who were occupying Mongolia. In the second quarter of the same century they started spreading westwards and conquered the entire steppe area up to the Aral, and their territory thus included the valley of the Ili up to the Balkhash, the valley of the Issiq-kul, the steppes of Chu and Chao, and the valley of the Jaxartes up to Aral. About 440 A. D., they occupied Sogdiana and Tokharestan. Balkh may have been occupied about the same time.

After the conquest of Balkh, the White Huns, under their king, Akhshunwar, invaded Khorasan in 484 and killed King Peroz. In the south they came into conflict with a branch of Kushans known as Kidara Kushans, after the name of their king Kidara, who were ruling in Tokharestan. Kidara and his son, Kungka, were also enemies of the Sassanian dynasty. After the Hephthalite victory against the Persian rulers the Kidarites found their position untenable in Balkh, crossed the Hindukush and settled down in the Kabul valley, after ousting the later Kushans from that region.

The Hephthalites, in the meantime, consolidated their position in Tokharestan, conquered Talekan, Merv and Herat and became a sort of protector of the Sassanian throne. They sent an embassy to China in 516. Soon after, they invaded Kabul, drove away the Kidara Kushans, and extended their dominion up to Gandhara.

Songyun, a Chinese envoy who came to Gandhara in 520, saw them there. The Huns subsequently crossed the Indus and invaded India. Although they suffered a crushing defeat in the hands of the Guptas about the middle of the 6th century A. D., they continued to rule in the Punjab and in Kashmir for about two generations, after which they were totally merged into the Indian population.

At the time when the Huns had entered India, their empire had reached the maximum extent and included the entire steppe from the upper Yulduz (north of Karasahr) to the Aral and Sogdiana, Merv, Eastern Iran, Afganistan and the Punjab. The Huns were allied by marriage ties, as can be ascertained from the account of the Chinese traveller, Songyun, with another nomadic tribe of Turkish origin called Juan-Juan.

TURKS

About this time a new power raised its head in Central Asia. They are the Turks, mentioned in the Chinese accounts as T'u-kiu i.e. Turkut, meaning "strong," They are known in Indian literature as Turushka. They were descendants of the ancient Hiung-nu race and had wolf as their totem, and were living towards the beginning of the 6th century in the region of Altai mountains as subjects of the Juan-Juans. The Juan-Juans became weak on account of a civil war between two chiefs, A-na-kwei and his uncle, Po-lo-men (520), and although the former came out victorious and became the sole master of the Juan-Juans, he now had to face the insubordination of his Turkish vassals.

One of the Turkish tribes called Kao-kiu in Chinese literature, and who were the same as Tolos, the ancestors of the Uigurs, were already in conflict with the Juan-Juans. Taking advantage of the weakness of the Juan-Juans they revolted against their domination in 521, but were defeated. They raised the standard of rebellion again in 546 but another Turkish tribe allied to them called T'u-kiu in Chinese history took the side of the Juan-Juans and suppressed them. Their chief, Bumin, asked for a Juan Juan princess in marriage as a price of his loyalty, but

A-na-kwei turned it down. This resulted in complete alienation of the Turks.

Bumin allied himself with the Turks of North China known in Chinese history as Si-wei (Toba) and crushed the Juan-Juan power in 552. Their remnants left the whole of Mongolia to the Turks and took refuge in China. Bumin now took the Imperial title of Qaghan and established his capital at Orkhon, but he died soon after (552). After Bumin's death, the empire was divided between his son and younger brother. His son, Mu-han, succeeded to the empire of Mongolia, of which the western limit extended to Hami region. Turkish hordes under him came to be known in history as the Eastern Turks. Mu-han had the Imperial title of Qaghan.

Bumin's younger brother Istami (She-tie-mi of Chinese accounts) became the chief of the western possessions of the Turks with the title Yabghu and the hordes under him came to be known in history as the Western Turks. The empire of the Western Turks comprised Zungaria, -- the valley of the Irtych, Imil, Yulduz basin, Illi region and the region of Chu and Talas. The summer capital of the Yabghu was at Yulduz and the winter capital on the bank of the Issiqul or in the valley of the Talas.

A formidable enemy of Istami in the immediate neighbourhood of his empire was the Hephthalite Huns, the former allies of the Juan-Juans. Istami therefore found it prudent to ally himself with Khosroes Anoshirvan, the Sassanian emperor of Persia to fight these common enemies. The combined Persian and Turkish forces destroyed the Hephthalites about 565, and forced their remnants to leave the region and migrate to Europe. The Hephthalite empire was now divided, Istami got Sogdiana and Khosroes got Bactriana. Bactriana was soon after annexed by Istami to his territories.

Istami's son Tardu was the Qaghan from 575 to 603. In 588 he invaded Tokharestan and went up to Herat. Tokharestan with its two capitals, Balkh and Kunduz came under Turkish possession in 597-598. When Hiuan-Tsang visited Tokharestan in 630 the country was under a *tegin* who was a vassal of the Turks. A Turkish Prince then resided at Kunduz.

A conflict started between the Eastern and Western Turks during the reign of Tardu and this ultimately weakened their hold in various regions of Central Asia. The chief of the Western Turks previously owed allegiance to the Qaghan of the Eastern Turks, but Tardu, in 582, ended this practice by assuming himself the title of Qaghan, and allying himself with China as against the Eastern Turks. The Qaghan of the Eastern Turks, Ishpara (Sha-po-lo) soon found himself attacked on the West by Tardu and in the East by the Kitans. Taking advantage of this situation the T'ang Emperor ultimately destroyed the power of the Eastern Turks and brought the Turkish chiefs under Chinese domination. The T'angs mantained good relations with the Western Turks.

Soon after 630 the Western Turks found themselves divided due to an internal disruption. The Qarluq tribe of the Western Turks revolted against the Qaghan She-hu and assassinated him. The Western Turks were now divided into two groups — Nu-she-pi in the West and S. W. of Issiqul and the Tu-lu in the North-West. The Tu-lu were defeated by the Chinese army posted at Hami in 641 and this led to the disintegration of the Khanat of the Western Turks for the time being.

In the third quarter of the 7th century Chinese power in Central Asia was on the wane. Tibetans occupied the Tarim basin in 670 and there was also a consequent resurgence of the Turks. The Nu-she-pi and Tu-lu tribes revolted against Chinese domination in 665. The Eastern Turks also rallied their power under the Qaghan Qutlugh. Qutlugh organized his people and consolidated his administration with the help of an adroit politician named Tonuqug who had his training in China.

Qutlugh started his campaigns against China in 682. The Chinese were harassed everywhere and ousted from ancient Turkish possessions. Qutlugh died in 691, but under his brother, Mo-ch'o (Bakchur) who ruled Turkestan under the title Qupagan-qaghan from 691 to 716, the policy of Qutlugh was followed against China. The Chinese were defeated everywhere and all the Turkish tribes, including the Nu-she-pi and Tu-lu, were brought under control, and a united Turkish empire was founded.

After Mo-ch'o's death in 716, succession was disputed for

a while. The son of Qutlugh killed Mo-ch'o's son, and set up his elder brother, Mo-ki-lien (Bilga Qaghan), on the throne. The latter reigned from 716 to 734. During this period war was successfully carried on against various tribes like the Toquz-Oguz, Toquz-Tatar, Uigur, Qarluq etc. and peaceful relations were established with China. Mo-ki-lien was poisoned in 731, and his death was followed by a series of troubles and by the destruction of the Eastern Turkish Empire in 744 by the Basmil tribes.

The Basmil tribes who destroyed the Eastern Turkish Empire failed, however, to set up an empire themselves. This work was left to the Uigurs. The Uigurs, with the help of another Turkish tribe named Qarluk, founded an empire which lasted for nearly a century (744-840). The architect of this new empire was the Uigur Khan, Qutlugh Bilga, who had his capital at Qarabalgasun on the Orkhon. Although Qutlugh Bilga died soon after the foundation of the Empire in 744 the empire remained strong till 840. During this period good relations were maintained with China, and, in fact, the Turks often played the part of protectors of the T'ang empire.

The Uigurs were ousted from Mongolia in 840 by the Kirghiz Turks, who came down from the region of Ienessei and occupied Qarabalgasun. Being driven from Mongolia, the Uigurs settled in the Tarim, Qara-Khodjo (Khocho), ancient Turfan, Dzimsa which became the Turkish Beshbaligh, Qarasahr and Kucha in 843. The Uigur kingdom of Beshbaligh-Kucha lasted till the 13th century and played an important part in the cultural history of the region.

THE INDO-EUROPEAN OASIS

In the history of the cultural exchange between China and Indo-Iranian world, it is the southern part of Central Asia which played the most important part. It was an area inhabited by Aryan-speaking people. We have already seen that the Yue-ches, the various branches of Scythians, the Wu-suns and other tribes which lived right up to Kansu were Aryans and evidently their migration had originated in the West. The civilisation of Chinese Turkestan up to about the 10th century was also mainly derived from India and Iran. This is why this region has been called by some scholars 'Indo-European oasis'. The late Sir Aurel Stein, that indefatigable explorer of Central Asian regions, preferred the name *Ser-India* which the ancient Greeks had used. The use of this name has the greatest justification for the simple reason that both China and India played a dominant role in shaping the civilisation of this area.

Ser-India is bounded on the north by the T'ien-shan or the Celestial Mountains and on the south by the Kun-lun ranges. On the east, this region is bounded by the Nan-shan which itself is a continuation of the Kun-lun. On the west, the Pamirs, the Imaos of the ancient Greek geographers, connect the T'ien-shan with the Hindu-kush.

These mountains give rise to important rivers, which flow towards the Taklamakan deserts, gradually dry up and ultimately lose themselves in the sands. The Kashgar Daria which rises from the T'ien-shan and the Yarkand Daria which rises from the Pamirs are powerful near their sources, but as they flow on, they gradually diminish in volume in the proximity of the deserts. These two combine together to form the Tarim river, which flows along the depression towards the marshes of the Lob-nor. This is the river which was mentioned in Indian literature as Sita. It is along these river basins that thickly populated and prosperous colonies had been established since very early times.

The colonies that flourished in the southern part of this region were from west to east — Cokkuka in the region of modern Yarkand, Śailadeśa in the region of Kashgar, Khotamna-Godana in the region of Khotan and Calmadana in the region of Cherchen. Smaller principalities also once existed in this region but they have now completely disappeared through the erosion of deserts. The ruins of old cities in the sand dunes are the only witness to their former existence.

In the northern part of this region, along the foot of the T'ien-shan, there were equally flourishing colonies. There were, from west to east — Bharuka in the region of modern Uch-Turfan, Kucirājya in the region of Kucha and Agnideśa in the region of

Karasahr. There is also evidence of early existence of small Indian colonies along the principal routes in these regions up to the frontier of China.

From very early times important trade routes passed through the Tarim basin from the frontier of China to the West. These are also known as the silk-routes as during the first few centuries of the Christian era traders carrying on trade by this route made a very profitable business in Chinese silk with the Roman countries in the West. Much racial conflict had taken place for centuries for controlling this important trade route between China and the West, and the Chinese emperors since the Han period had taken great pains in guarding these routes of Eastern Turkestan.

There were two routes passing through the Tarim basin from the frontiers of China up to Balkh. From about the first century A. D. they were used not only for trade between China and the West but also for the dissemination of Buddhist culture from the West to the states of Eastern Turkestan and to China. Thereafter they became predominantly 'Buddhist routes' and were used for cultural exchange till about the 11th century.

The two principal routes parted from Tun-huang, in the province of Kan-su : one passed by the gate of Yu-men-kuan towards the north-west, and the other by that of Yang-kuan directly west-ward.

Tun-huang, we know, played a great part in the history of China's relation with the West. Like Purusapura (Peshawar), situated on the highway leading to the undefined West, Tun-huang came to be a meeting place of foreigners, from the beginning of the Christian era. Already in the middle of the second century, the Buddhist pilgrims found a place of shelter there on their way towards the capital of China. In the third century A. D. we hear of Indian families settled down in Tun-huang. It had already become a great centre of Buddhist missionaries at that time. During the centuries following, the Wei dynasty, the great patron of Buddhism and Buddhist art, determined to bring about a transformation of the place, so important for the diffusion of Buddhistic culture. It was at this time that the construction of Buddhist temples began and grottos were scooped out in the surrounding rocks. The number of grottos were multiplied until there was a thousand of them containing many works of art and statues of Buddha. It is these grottos of Ts'ien-fo-t'ong, long fallen in oblivion, that cherished silently for about a thousand years a wonderful library of the middle ages. The vast number of manuscripts it contained, discovered mostly by the French archaeological mission of Pelliot, show amply what a great centre of learning Tun-huang was in the glorious time of the T'ang dynasty. The diversity of the languages, in which these manuscripts exist, Kuchean, Khotanese, Syriac, Tibetan, Sanskrit, etc., show that Tun-huang was really a great meeting place of China and the West.

The southern route starting from Tun-huang passed by the gate of Yang-kuan and proceeding westward reached the country of Shan-shan (to the south of Lob-nor). From Shan-shan it went along the course of the river Tarim up to So-kiu (Yarkand) and crossing the Pamir (Kizil rabat) reached the country of the Yue-che (Balkh) and Parthia (Ngan-si). The route of the North, passed by Kiue-she (Turfan), the ancient capital of the kingdom of Lou-lan ; it followed the Tarim right up to the west to Shu-lei (Kashgar) and continued across the Pamir (Kizil art) up to the country of Ta-wan (Ferganah), K'ang-kiu (Sogdiana) and other countries in the valley of the Oxus.

But the route to India followed a little different course. Fa-hien, the first Chinese pilgrim to India, notices in detail the way he followed from China to India. Starting from Ch'ang-ngan in 399 A. D., with other monks he passed by the principal localities of the province of Kan-su, viz. Lan-chou, Leang-chou, Kan-chou, Su-chou and Tun-huang and arrived at Shan-shan to the south of Lob-nor. They visited the countries of Yen-ki (Karasahr), Yu-tien (Khotan), Tseu-ho (Karghalik), Kiuan-yu-mo (Tash-kurghan) and Kie-ch'a (Kashgar). They passed by To-li (Darel, in Dardistan) and then, crossing the mountains, reached the valley of Gilgit which leads to the region of the Indus.

A century later Song Yun visited India. He has left us a

fairly detailed account of the route he followed on his way to India. It is also the southern route which he followed up to the Pamir region. From Tash-kurghan (Tsiu-mo), however, he went to Pa-ho (Wakhan) and passed by Po-che (the mountainous region to the north of Chitral) to She-mi (Chitral). But instead of following the route of Gilgit to Kashmir, he directed his course southwards to Udyana, in the valley of the Swat and then to Gandhara (Peshawar).

Hiuan Tsang in 629 followed the northern route. From Kan-su he went to Kao-chang (Yarkhoto, near Turfan); then he visited the countries of A-ki-ni (Karasahr). Kiu-che (Kucha) Po-lu-kia (Yaka-aryk), to the south of the T'ien-shan; he crossed the T'ien-shan by the Bedal pass, and passed by the north bank of Issiqul, where he met the Tokmak Turks. Shortly before the arrival of Hiuan Tsang, the country had been visited by an Indian monk of Nalanda, Prabhakaramitra, who went to China later on to receive the highest honour from the Emperor of China. Hiuan Tsang then passed by Sogdiana, crossed "the Iron Gates" to the south of Kesch (Sahahr-i-sabz) and reached the country of Tokharestan. The capital of the country was at that time at Huo (Kunduz) to the south of the Oxus. Hiuan Tsang descended by the pass of Bamyan to the valley of Kapisa. Twenty years later, on his way back to China, he followed the southern route. From Kapisa he crossed the Hindukush by the valley of Panjshir, and reached Kunduz. He then passed by Badakshan (Pa-to-ch'uang-na), Ying-po-kien (Yamgan, the valley of the Koksha), and Hun-t'o-lo (Kandut). Then crossing the Pamir, he visited the countries of Tash-kurghan (Kie-pan-t'o) Kia-she (Kasghar). Che-kiu kia (Karghalik) and Kiu-sa-tan-na (Khotan). From Khotan, he followed the usual route by the south of Lob-nor to Ch'ang-ngan, the capital.

The last Chinese pilgrim who has left a somewhat detailed notice of the route he followed for going to India by Eastern Turkestan, is Wu-k'ong. He left China in 751 A. D. as the head of an official mission sent to the kingdom of Kapisa in order to bring back a Chinese ambassador. Wu-k'ong passed by Kucha, which was at that time the seat of the protectorate of Ngan-si, Su-lei (Kashgar), the five Ch'e-ni (Shighnan) of the Po-mi (Pamir) and the Hu-mi (Wakhan), and reached the Indus region by the valley of Yasin and Gilgit, known as Po-lu-lo (Bolor), the most frequented route for entering India. Wu-k'ong visited Udyana (Valley of the Swat) and Kapisa. He followed a little different route on his way back to China. He passed by Ku-tu (Khottal), Kiu-mi-che (Kumedh, now Karategin), Ch'e-ni (Shighnan), and reached Su-lei (Kashgar), and then Yu-t'ien (Khotan). He passed by Wei-jong (Yaka-aryak), Kiue tseu (Kucha), Yen-ki (Karasahr) and Pei-t'ing (Tsi-mou-sa, near Ku-ch'eng) and returned to Ch'ang-ngan in 790 A. D.

The ancient silk route had another section, the western one, which connected the Roman orient with Balkh during the early centuries of the Christian era. From Balkh it passed to Antioch, the capital of Syria, through Merv, Hecatompylos (Raghes near Teheran), Ecbatana (Hamadhan), and Hieropolis (Menbidj) on the Euphrates. The Persian empire therefore had a share in the silk trade with the Roman countries, and we have seen that this often brought her in conflict with the Central Asian nomads. But the cultural exchange between various nations during almost a millennium along the 'silk route' throws into background their commercial interest.

CHAPTER II

TOKHARESTAN AND EASTERN IRAN

HISTORICAL BACKGROUND

The first country of Central Asia on the threshold of the Indian cultural world was Tokharestan, the land of the Tukhāras. It was the melting pot of various nomadic civilizations that passed from the North to the South and from the East to the West at different times during the historical period. It was also the land where the nomads had their first training in modes of settled life before they moved on to other lands. Tokharestan, therefore, was an active intermediary between India on one side and Iran and Turan on the other. It was the Tukhāra people who carried the elements of Indian culture and religion to the North and the East, and also transmitted the cultures of Iran, Greece and the nomads to India. Tokharestan thus played a very important part in the history of India's cultural relations with Central Asia.

Although in the Mahomedan period Tokharestan came to mean the territories between Badakshan and Balkh, in the earlier period it was used in a much broader geographical sense, and embraced all the provinces on both banks of the Amu Darya (Oxus) which were economically dependent on Balkh. It extended up to the passes of the Hindukush. In the middle of the 7th century, the boundaries of Tokharestan as described by Hiuan-tsang were : 'the Iron Pass', (Derbent near Badakshan) in the North, the Snow mountains or the Hindukush in the South, Persia, in the West and the Ts'ung-ling or the Pamirs in the East'. Thus, on the North it bounded on Sogdiana (ancient Sugdik, Sulik, modern Samarcand) and on the East on Eastern Turkestan. The river Oxus flowed through the country.

The ancient Chinese Annals of the Han period refer to the country as Ta-hia. China first established contact with Ta-hia in the 2nd century B. C. The ancient pronunciation of the Chinese name was approximately *D'at-g'a, which may have been a transcription of an old form of the name like *Dogar (Tokhar —, Tukhāra). Although some uncertainty hangs about this equation, there is no doubt that geographically Ta-hia corresponded to Tokharestan of later times. Indian literature of about the same period knows the name of the Tukharas. The Ramayana mentions them as Tukhāra. The name is given in the same form in the Mahabharata and such Buddhist texts as the Saddharmasmrityupasthana and the Mahamayuri. The Puranas mention it either as Tukhāra or as Tuṣāra just because *ṣa* was pronounced as *kh* in ancient Sanskrit. The Greek and Latin writers also had a knowledge of these people. Pliny mentions them as Thochari, Ptolemy as Thagouroi and Periegetes and all later writers as Tochari. The Chinese sources from the beginning of the 4th century onwards speak of the country as T'u-ho-lo (*T'u-xuo-la), i. e. Tukhara. The Tibetans knew them as Thogar or Thodgar. In a still later period the Uigurs speak of them as Toxri and their country as Twxrstn, i. e. Tokharestan.

The Chinese historical annals throw considerable light on the political vicissitudes of the country from the second century before Christ. The country was inhabited by the Sakas, whom the Chinese call Sai (Sek), who were a branch of the Iranian people and spoke a North Iranian dialect. Since the foundation of the Bactrian empire of the Greeks in the middle of the 3rd century B. C. the southern part of their territory must have passed into the hands of the Greeks, but they were still maintaining their independence in the North. It was the thrust of another nomadic people which obliged them to quit their land.

A very powerful people whom the Chinese call Ta Yue-che or Great Yue-che once occupied the southern and eastern parts of the Tarim basin, and had settled down on the Western frontier of China in the region of Tunhuang in the modern province of Kan-su. They were attacked by the Hiung-nus or the Huns who came from the north, were completely defeated by them in 176 B. C. and were forced to quit the region. Moving westwards in search of new lands, they ultimately came to Ta-hia or Tokharestan about 160 B. C. and conquered the land from the Sakas. The Sakas then moved southwards and entered Kashmir by the Bolor route. The Great Yue-ches, now undisputed masters of Tokharestan, took to a settled life and gradually set up an empire with which even China was soon anxious to establish friendly relations with a view to fight more effectively the Huns, who were still making inroads into the Chinese empire. The first Chinese ambassador Chang-kien came to the Yue-che country for that purpose in 125 B. C.

The Great Yue-ches, after the conquest of Ta-hia, divided the kingdom into five principalities: Hiu-mi, Shuang-mi, Kui-shuang, Hi-tun and Tu-mi, each under a chief called Hi-hou (i. e. Yabghu) for the purpose of administration. About a century later, one of these chiefs, the *hi-hou* of Kui-shuang carried out a successful revolution, conquered the other four and laid the foundation of one of the most powerful empires. This chief is called K'ieu-tsieu-k'io-(*K'ieu-dz'ieu-kiap), i. e. Kuju Kapa or Kujulo Kadphises of history. After consolidating his position in Tokharestan, Kujulo Kadphises invaded Ngan-si (Parthian empire), Kao-fu (Kabul region), P'u-ta (Bak-ta, Bactria) and Ki-pin (Kasmira-Gandhara), and founded a great empire. He died at the age of more than 80 and was succeeded by his son Yen-kao-chen (correct form Yen-kao-mi) i. e. Vema Kapi—Wema Kadphises. Wema further added T'ien-chu (India) to his empire and governed it through an agent. The Chinese Annals tell us clearly that these kings were known as the kings of Kui-shuang (i. e. Kushan) but the Chinese continued to call them Ta Yue-che according to their old practice. It is not clear whether the Kushans ethnically belonged to the Yue-che stock or not, but there is no doubt that they were Tukhara. The Indian sources, specially the Puranas which give dynastic lists of Kushan rulers, call them Tukhara.

Tokharestan seems to have been under the rule of the Kushans till the middle of the 5th century. They are still mentioned in the Chinese Annals under the name Great Yue-che. It is said in the Annals of the Northern dynasties (Pei-she) that their king Ki-to-lo (Kidara) was obliged by the attacks of the Juan-Juan to migrate to the city of Po-lo (B'ak-la-Bactra) or Balkh and it was at this time that he annexed Gandhara to his territory. During the period 424-451 a number of merchants of Tokharestan (the country of the Great Yue-che) went to the Chinese capital and taught the Chinese the secret of polychrom glass manufacture. The Kidara Kushans, even after their transfer to Balkh and Gandhara, sent embassies to China in 477 and 511. Kidara, and later his son, Kungkas, waged war against the Sassanian king, Peroz (459- 484). After the Hephthalite victory over Peroz, the Kidara Kushans under Kungkas moved to the Kabul region, where they were later exterminated by the same Hephthalites.

In fact, Tokharestan had passed into the hands of the White Huns or the Hephthalites in the meantime. They had occupied the Oxus valley towards the middle of the 5th century, forcing the Kidarites to migrate first to Balkh and ultimately to Gandhara. The Chinese call these White Huns 'Hoa' who had got mixed up with the Juan-Juans. After their occupation of Tokharestan they became a formidable enemy of the Persian empire. In 484, their king Akhschounwar won a victory over the Sassanian ruler Peroz, who was killed in the battle. The Chinese historians tell us that the name of the royal family was Ye-t'a or Ye-t'ai-yi-li-t'o — *Hephthal*, and hence the name of the tribe. The Hephthalite empire, we have already seen, was first confined toTokharestan, but it soon extended in different directions. Between 502 and 556 it included Kapisa (Kabul Valley), Karasahr, Kucha, Kashgar, Sogdiana and Khotan. It also included the states of the Pamir regions : Tashkurghan, Wakhan and Chitral, and extended up to Gandhara.

The Western Turks appeared on the scene towards the middle of sixth century. They first defeated the Juan-Juans, who were the ally and overlord of the Hephthalites and then destroyed the Hephthalite empire. Tokharestan was conquered from the Hephthalites by the Western Turks in 588-589, and its two capital cities Balkh and Kunduz were taken by them in 597-98. When Hiuan Tsang visited the country in 630, Tokharestan was under a Turkish Governor, a prince of the blood with the title *tegin* who had his headquarters at Kunduz. The Western Turks suffered defeat in the hands of the Chinese in 557, and since then a Chinese suzerainty was accepted by them. The Chinese helped the Turkish Governor of Tokharestan between 656 and

660 in an administrative reorganisation of the country. The country was divided into 24 administrative units, which must have been the old districts reorganised afresh.

Tokharestan had cordial diplomatic relations with China till 759. Embassies were sent to China with presents many times between 705 and 759. The Chinese sources tell us that the ruler of the country from 742 to 755 was Yabghu She-li Mang-kia-lo (Srí-Mangala), who repulsed an attack of the Tibetans and Khasas with the help of military help sent from Kucha, probably by the Chinese. The last ambassador to China was sent in 759. His name is recorded as U-li-to (Udita ?). In spite of Turkish domination, the various states of Tokharestan maintained some sort of autonomy, and after the subsequent Arab conquest the indigenous dynasties continued to exist for sometime.

GEOGRAPHICAL SITUATION

The geographical structure of Tokharestan divided the country into a number of small states. We are told by the Chinese sources that the Great Yue-ches, after their conquest of the country, divided it into 25 principalities for the purpose of administration. Although the names occur in the Chinese records, it is difficult to identify them in the present state of our knowledge.

Later on, at the time of the rise of the Kushan power, the country was divided amongst the chiefs of five important principalities : Hiu-mi, with its capital at Ho-mo, Shuang-mi with its capital at Shuang-mi, Kui-shuang with its capital at Hu-tsao, Hi-tun with its capital at Po-mao, and Tu-mi, which seem to have been almost identical with Kao-fu of later sources, with its capital at Kao-fu (Kabul region).

It appears from a study of the Chinese Annals that these were the original divisions of the country before the Yue-ches took possession of it. In spite of their administrative arrangement, each of the principalities was an autonomous state, and later on it was the chief of the Kui-shuang who led a successful revolt and founded a new empire, after destroying all other powers within the country.

Even after the loss of the Indian empire the Kushans maintained their authority on the kingdom of Tokharestan till the time of the Hephthalite invasion. Under the Hephthalites also the small kingdoms must have maintained some sort of autonomy, and the same sort of political condition still prevailed under the Turks. The political condition of the country is very clearly described by Hiuan-tsang in the middle of the 7th century when the Turks were effective rulers of the land. In spite of Turkish domination, the country remained divided into 27 principalities, most of which were visited by the pilgrim.

Hiuan-tsang tells us that the royal race had been extinct for many centuries, and that in his time each of the 27 states, which were divided by natural boundaries, was under a chief who was ruling independently. The country as a whole was dependent on the Turks. Hiuan-tsang divides the country into two zones, the western and the eastern. The western zone consisted of the sixteen states from Ta-mi (Termez) to Kie-chin (Gaz) covering the whole country from the Iron Pass (Derbent) to Gaz, the most fertile zone of the Oxus valley. He visited these states on his way to India. The Eastern zone consisted of the other states, mostly mountainous, beginning with An-ta-lo-fo (Anderab), which he visited in course of his return journey from India towards Kashgar. All these mountainous states are described by the pilgrim as "the ancient" Tu-ho-lo (Tukhara) country. It is not certain what he exactly means by it. From the description of the people and their writing and literature, it is clear that he does not mean that these states had been abandoned by the Tukhara people in his times. He probably means that these had gone directly under the Turkish domination, while the Western states were still preserving some sort of autonomy.

The principalities mentioned by Hiuan-tsang are also known from later sources, specially from the works of the Muslim geographers of the 10th century — such as Abu Zayd al-Balkhi (d. 934) of Balkh, Istakhri (d. 951) and Maqdisi (d. 985). The principalities mentioned by pilgrims may not be the original administrative divisions of Tokharestan under the Yue-ches, but they could not have been much different. These divisions were :

(1) *Ta-mi*, mentioned in later Chinese sources as T'e-rh-mi is ancient Demetria of the Bactrian Greeks, Tirmidh, Termed or Termez of modern times. The ruins of the ancient city are found on the Northern bank of the Oxus.

(2) *Chi-kia-yen-na* — Chi-han-na or Shi-han-na of later Chinese sources identified with Caghaniyan or Saghaniyan on the Surkhab. The rulers of pre-Muslim times are mentioned by the Moslem writers as Caghan-Khudhah.

(3) *Hu-lu-mo* — which was reached by Hiuan-tsang going eastwards from Caghaniyan. It is identified with Akhrun or Kharum near the junction of the Kafirnihan and Surkhab.

(4) *Su-man* — to the east of Kharum and identified with Shuman.

(5) *Ku-ho-yen-na* — to the south-west of Shuman, identified with Kawadhiyan (Kawalikan) i. e. Karategin on the Oxus.

(6) *Huo-sha* — to the east of Karategin, identified with Waksh.

(7) *Ku-tu-lo* — to the east of Waksh, identified with Khottalan which extended up to the Pamirs.

(8) *Ku-mi-t'o* — to the east of Khottalan, situated in the Pamirs, identified with Komed. In the T'ang Annals it is mentioned as Ku-mi and by Wu-k'ong as Kiu-mi-che. The Muslim writers mention it as Kumed or Kumadh. Maqdisi says that the country was inhabited by a people called Kumiji supposed to be of Turkish origin. The name has been connected with Komedon, Cambothi, Kambuson of the Greek writers and Kamboja of the Indian literature.

(9) *Fo-ka-lang* — to the south-west of Komed, identified with Baghlan to the south of Kunduz.

(10) *Kie-lu-shi-min-kan* — to the south of Baghlan and identified with Rub and Simingan.

(11) *Hu-lin* — to the north-west of Simingan, identified with Khulm.

(12) *Fo-ho* — to the west of Khulm and identified with Balkh on the south bank of the Oxus.

(13) *Yue-mei-t'o* — to the south-west of Balkh and identified with Zumathan.

(14) *Hu-si-kan* — to the south-west of Zumathan and identified with Gozgan.

(15) *Ta-la-kan* — to the north-west of Gozgan, identified with Taleqan which, in the Muslim period, was the largest city in Tokharestan, being one-third of the size of Balkh.

(16) *Kie-chin* — south of Balkh, identified with Gaz or Darral-Gaz.

Besides these states Hiuan-tsang mentions a few others which he visited on his return journey, and which he mentions as the old Tukhara country. It is not clear whether they were politically dependent on Tokharestan in his times, but they no doubt belonged to the ethnic and cultural zone of Tokharestan. We know that some of them were in earlier times integral parts of Tokharestan. These states are the following :

(1) *An-ta-lo-fo* — identified with Anderab. The pilgrim describes the country as a hilly region with fertile valleys possessing both Deva temples and Buddhist monasteries with monks of the Mahasanghika school. He also saw an Asokan stupa in the country.

(2) *K'uo-si-to* — to the north-west of Anderab where the pilgrim saw three Buddhist monasteries. It is the same as Khost of Baber and Khust of modern times.

(3) *Huo* — to the north-west of Khost. The pilgrim tells us that the states had no separate rulers, but was under the Turkish king who ruled over the small states south of the Iron Pass. The country was on the south bank of the Oxus and extended up to the Pamirs in the east. There were ten Buddhist monasteries in the capital with a few hundred monks of both Hinayana and Mahayana. Huo, which is mentioned in some Chinese texts as Kuah, is said to have been the name of a tribe. It is identified with Kunduz of Baber and Warwaliz of modern times.

(4) *Mang-kan* — to the east of Kunduz in the Pamirs and a state under Badakshan in the time of Hiuan-tsang — modern Mungkan.

(5) *A-li-ni* — to the north of Mungkan, which lay along the Oxus -- identified with Arhang.

(6) *Ho-lo-hu* — to the east of Mungkan, identified with Ragh or Raghwan between Kokcha and the Oxus — dependent on Badakshan.

(7) *Ki-li-si-mo* — Kism, to the east of Mungkan.

(8) *Po-li-ho* (Bolor ?) — to the east of Mungkan.

(9) *Hi-mo-to-lo* — to the east of Kism. The pilgrim tells us that the rulers of the coutry were of the Sakya race — claiming descent from one of the four Sakya princes driven out of Kapilavastu for having fought against Virudhaka against the advice of Buddha. The customs of the people as described by the pilgrim remind one of the Hephthalites. The women, like the Hephthalite women, had a long wooden head-dress with two horns, one representing the father-in-law and the other the mother-in-law. The name has been restored as Hephthal (from Hema — Hevatala).

(10) *Po-to-ch'ang-na* — to the east of Hematala — the king in the time of Hiuan-tsang was a devout Buddhist — there were 4 Buddhist monasteries with a few monks in the city. It has been identified with Badakshan of which the capital was situated near modern Faizabad.

(11) *Yin-po-kien* — Yamgan, modern Yambakan.

(12) *Ku-lang-na* — to the south-east of the former, identified with modern Karran.

(13) *Ta-mo-si-t'ie-ti* — to the north-east of Karran, identified with ancient Dar-i-Mastin (Mastag) i. e. modern Wakhan.

Very important trade routes passed through these states. First of all the trade route *that connected Badakshan and Little Tibet* of the Upper Indus valley passed through Yamgan, Karran, Wakhan and Shughnan. Badakshan was famous for its mines of lapis lazuli and ruby and its capital was situated near modern Fyzabad. Tibetan musk was prized in these states and it passed through this trade route. The states from Badakshan up to Shughnan did not submit to Islam till the 11th century. Even in the 10th century they are described by the Muslim geographers as heathens (Buddhists). The other important route was from *Badakshan to Balkh*, the route followed by Hiuan-tsang and many other travellers going to India. From Badakshan it passed through Taleqan, Warwaliz (Kunduz), and Khulm to Balkh. This was the most frequented route to the Hindukush. From Khulm southwards the route passed by Simingan, which was probably situated near modern Haybak, and Baghlan to Anderab. In the east, *Shughnan was connected with Eastern Turkestan* by another important route, which passed by Shang-mi (Chitral), Kie-pan-to (Sarikol), and Wu-sha (Yangi-Hisar, Yarkand).

This geographical position of Tokharestan with all its principal trade routes clearly shows its importance in early history.

LANGUAGE AND LITERATURE

There has been a great controversy on the language spoken in ancient Tokharestan, and it cannot be said that a definite conclusion has been arrived at in regard to this problem. A good deal of progress, however, has been made in clearing the issue, and a very probable theory has been formulated about the language and literature of these ancient people by Prof. P. Pelliot. About the language and literature of Tu-ho-lo (Tokharestan) Hiuan-tsang says :

"The number of radical letters in their language is 25 ; by combining these they express all objects around them. Their writing is across the page, and they read from left to right. The literary records have increased gradually, and exceed those of the people of Su-li (Sogdiana)".

The zone of Tukhara influence in language and literature seems to have extended up to its natural frontiers to the upper Kabul valley. About the language and literature of Bamiyan the pilgrim says :

"The literature, customary rules, and money used in commerce are the same as those of the Tukhara country. Their language is a little different".

About Kapisa (Kafiristan) also the pilgrim says :

"Their written language was very like that of Tukhara, but the customs, spoken language and doctrinal rules were different".

In the Pamir region, the two states of She-ki-ni (Shughnan) and Shang-mi (Chitral) had also, according to Hiuan-tsang, writing similar to that of the Tukharas, although their language was somewhat different. Further to the East, beginning from Kie-p'an-to (Wakhan), all states belonged in this regard to the sphere of Kashgarian influence.

From the evidence of Hiuan-tsang it is therefore clear that practically the whole of Tokharestan and the adjoining states in tae Hindukush and Pamir regions had the same writing and literary language even up to the middle of the 7th century. The writing was horizontal, read from left to right, and had 25 radical letters and probably a few more derivatives.

It is quite likely that the alphabet used in Tokharestan was adopted from the Brahmi. The fragments of literary documents discovered in the Northern part of the Tarim basin, specially Kucha and Karasahr, have brought to light the remains of a new language which, according to certain scholars, is the ancient language of Tokharestan. The writing in these documents is a modified form of Brahmi suited to the phonetic needs of the language and contains about 25 basic letters of the Brahmi alphabet if we exclude the secondary forms.

The existence of the ancient language of Tokharestan has been attested by some Uigur texts. One of these texts, which is the fragment of the translation of a very large work called *Maitreya-samiti* has the following colophon :

> "End of the 10th section entitled — the descent of Bodhisattva Maitreya from the Tuṣita heaven on earth — of the holy book Maitrisamit (Maitreyasamiti) translated from the language of India (anätkak) into the Toxri language by the teacher vaibazaki (vaibhāṣika) acarya Āriacintri (Āryacandra) and translated from the Toxri language into the Turkish (turk) by the teacher Prtaniarakst (Prajñārakṣita)."

From this colophon it is clear that the original Maitreyasamiti was in Sanskrit, from which it was translated into *Toxri* or the language of the Tokharians, and from the Toxri it was again translated into Turk Uigur.

Although the Uigur version of the Maitreyasamiti does not give a clear idea of the Toxri language, we get a number of fragments of the Maitreyasamiti in one of the ancient and hitherto unknown languages from northern part of Eastern Turkestan. This unknown language which has been variously described by scholars as Dialect I, Tokharian A, Karsahrian, Agnean etc. may be tentatively identified with the ancient language of Tokharestan i. e. Toxri or Thocari. We may even call it the language of the Kushans as the latter were Tukhara or Tochari proper. This language was an independent branch of the Indo-European family of language, having no direct connection with the Indo-Iranian. It had two dialects so far as we can know from the ancient documents, the second dialect usually called Tokharian B was current in the Northern part of Eastern Turkestan in the region of Kucha and Karasahr.

Unfortunately no remains of the Tokharian literature have been discovered from Tokharestan proper. They have been found mostly in the region of Karasahr and Turfan along with Uigur documents. The reason is not, however, far to seek. Since the 7th century, the Turks had been in contact with Tokharestan. We have seen that in the times of Hiuan-tsang the states of Tokharestan were under the suzerainty of the Turks. The Turks, as we shall see later, had been initiated to Buddhism in Tokharestan. The Uigur branch of the Turks founded a new empire in the region of Turfan in the 9th century, and it was then that they started having a Buddhist canon. It was the Tokharian literature alone which was available to them in the 9th century. Other Buddhist countries in Eastern Turkestan were in decadence. So the Tokharian priests must have sought asylum in the newly founded Turkish empire, being driven by the Muslim conquerors of Tokharestan. This is just the reason for which we get the Tokharian documents only in the region of Turfan and Karasahr. We know also from the Muslim sources that such literature was available in Tokharestan in the beginning of the Arab rule. Samani tells us that Khottalan and adjoining states had a special alphabet and books written in it.

The nature of the ancient Tokharian language and the remains of its literature will be more fully discussed later in connection with the history of the region where they have been actually found i. e. Kucha and Karasahr in the northern part of the Tarim basin.

But we get some sure remains of the old language of Tokharestan proper from various sources. The early Chinese texts tell us that in the time of Chang-kien (2nd cent. B. C.) India was called by the people of Tokharestan *Indak* (which is the correct ancient pronunciation of Chinese name Shen-tu). The Kushans were Tukharas, and they used on their coins evidently certain Tokharian forms of the names of divinities — *Boddo* (Buddha), *Oado* (Vāta) and *Oesho* (Iśa). The famous Buddhist stupa of Kanishka in Peshawar is called in Chinese *tsio-li*, which was a transcription of a word like *cakrik*. This, according to Pelliot, is a Tokharian word meaning stupa or temple. In fact, in some of the Pamir dialects, Yagnobi, Ormuri etc. the word for temple is still Cakka, Cuki, Sakek etc.

Tokharians were intermediaries between India and Iran, and it is likely that the old Persian loan words from Sanskrit were often based on Tokharian forms of the words; in fact they may be more easily explained on the basis of such an assumption. Some of the old Persian loans are *Bidpai* (from Sanskrit Vidyāpati), *Kalalak-Damanak* (Karaṭaka-Damanaka) *bilaur* (vaidurya), *sakar* (śarkarā), *nilopal* (nīlotpala), *catrang* (caturanga), *vanjak* (vaṁśaka), *But* (Buddha), etc. Some of these words as found in Tokharian of about the 6th cent. A. D. such as *Pud* for Buddha, *sakar* for śarkarā and *nilopal* for *nīlotpala* show that the bases of the Persian loans might have been Tokharian, not of the Kushan period, but of the later period, i. e. post-Kushan (300-700 A. D.)

BUDDHIST CULTURE

Buddhism was the predominant religion in the various states of Tokharestan from about the 2nd century B. C. up to the beginning of the 8th century, when it was conquered by the Arabs. A legend recorded by Hiuan-tsang tells us that the first two lay disciples of Buddha, Trapusa and Bhallika were responsible for introducing Buddhism in that country. According to it, the two merchants were natives of the kingdom of Balhika. Probably the name of one of them, Bhalluka or Bhallika is connected with the name of the country. They had gone to India for trade, and happened to be at Bodhgaya when the Buddha had just attained his enlightenment. They offered him cakes and honey out of their provision and became his first lay disciples. Buddha, at the time of their departure, gave them his hair and nail-cuttings. On their return home they built stupas on these relics. Hiuan-tsang mentions these stupas in the neighbourhood of the city of Balkh. Whatever may be the value of this legend, there seems to be no doubt that Buddhism was carried to Balkh in the time of Asoka. Asoka speaks of his efforts to introduce Buddhism among the people of Gandhara, Kamboja and Yona. The three peoples were neighbours. Kambojas, we have seen, were probably a branch of the Tukhara people. The Yonas were no doubt the Greeks of Bactria. It is not known what progress Buddhism made after its first introduction. But soon after Asoka, Demetrius, in conjunction with Menander, seems to have taken up arms in the defence of Buddhism, and its authorised patrons, the descendents of Asoka. The Great Yue-ches also, after their conquest of Tokharestan, adopted this new faith. The Kushans became great patrons of Buddhism. The first inflow of Buddhist culture to China was from Tokharestan. It was in the year 2 B. C. that the Chinese ambassador Tsing Kiang received Buddhist texts as presents to the Chinese Court.

We know of two famous Buddhist scholars of Tokharestan who worked in the Kushan period. One of them was Ghoṣaka, who is definitely described as a Tukhara. He took an important part in the compilation of the Vibhāṣā, a stupendous commentary of the Abhidharmapiṭaka of the Sarvastivada school, which was compiled in the Buddhist council of Purusapura (Peshawar) convoked by Kanishka. Discussions on abstruse subjects by great Buddhist scholars of the time were held under the supervision of Pārśva, and we know that Ghoṣaka took an important part in that discussion. He also composed an original treatise on Abhidharma—the Abhidharmāmṛta which is preserved in Chinese translation, of the third century. It is one of the most clear expositions of the Abhidharma doctrines. It is said that after completing his work at the council of Purusapura, Ghoṣaka returned to his own country (aparanta). Ghosaka was thus a follower of the Vibhasa, and belonged to what is usually known as the Vaibhasika school. In course of time, the Vaibhasika school had different sub-schools, and one of them was called Pascatya or Western Vaibhasika, which was connected with the country of Balhika. Possibly the tradition of this school goes back to Ghosaka. We know even from later sources that Balkh was a great centre of original Buddhist studies. Hiuan-tsang says that the Navasangharama of Balhika was "the only Buddhist establishment north of the Hindukush, in which there was a constant succession of Masters who were commentators of the canon". The importance of the Vaibhasika school of the Tukhara country is also brought out by the remains of Tokharian literature. We have already seen that Aryacandra, who first translated the Maitreyasamiti into the Tokharian language, was a Vaibazika—Vaibhasika.

The Tanjur section of the Tibetan Buddhist Canon has preserved the translation of a work entitled *Vinayasūtraṭikā*, which was the work of Dharmamitra, a Vaibhasika Acarya of the Tukhara country. In the colophon of the text it is further said that Dharmamitra was a native of Tarmita (Termez) on the Paksu (Oxus).

A very important contribution was made by the Buddhist monks of the Yue-che country, i. e. Tokharestan, towards the spread of Buddhist culture in China. Chinese literature distinguishes these monks by prefixing the word Che-(from Yue-che) to their names. The first two missionaries to China in 68 A. D., Kasyapa Matanga and Dharmaratna, were met by the Chinese ambassadors in the country of the Yue-ches. A monk of rare learning of Tukhara origin named Lokaksema went to Loyang in 147 A. D., and translated there some of the most important texts of the Buddhist canon into Chinese. Lokaksema worked in China till 188. Some of his translations are still extant. Towards the end of the same century (190-220), one of his young disciples, Che Kien, who was also of Tukhara origin, was compelled to leave North China on account of political trouble and settle at Nanking, where he worked till the middle of the 3rd century A. D. He translated over a hundred Buddhist texts, 49 of which still exist.

Another Buddhist monk named Dharmaraksa (Chinese name—Fa-hu), who was born of a Tukhara family, settled in Tunhuang towards the middle of the 3rd century A. D., had travelled far and wide in Central Asia and had learnt, we are told, 36 different languages. He went to China in 284 A. D., and worked there till 313. He translated nearly two hundred Buddhist texts into Chinese, and 90 of them still exist. A Tukhara monk named She-lun came to China in 373 and translated 4 works into Chinese. The last of the Tukhara monks to be mentioned in the Chinese sources was Dharmanandi, who went from the Tukhara country to China in 384 and translated a number of works into Chinese, two of which, including *Ekottaragama*, are still found.

We have no systematic record on the condition of Buddhism in the early period in Tokharestan and adjoining countries. Hiuan-tsang alone gives us a somewhat complete description of Buddhism in the country. In his times, almost in every state there were some Buddhist monasteries with a few monks, but in the cities of Ta-mi (Termez), Fo-ho (Balkh), Kie-chi (Gaz) and Huo (Kunduz) the condition of Buddhism was the most prosperous. In Termez there were 10 monasteries with nearly 1,000 monks, in Gaz about 10 monasteries with about 100 monks, and in Kunduz also about 10 monasteries with a few hundred monks. In Kunduz the monks belonged to both Hinayana and Mahayana, whereas in Gaz they were all Hinayanists of the Sarvastivada school. In Anderab there was a number of monasteries with monks of the Mahasanghika school. But Balkh was the most important centre of Buddhism in the whole country. Hiuan-tsang speaks of nearly 100 monasteries with more than 3,000 monks. We know that Buddhism was already decadent in the time of Hiuan-tsang. That makes it probable that the number of monasteries and monks was still larger in earlier times.

Hiuan-tsang gives a vivid description of the Buddhist establishments of Balkh. He tells us that the city was known as Little Rājagṛha, probably on account of its importance in the Buddhist world, being second to Rājagṛha of Magadha in the eyes of local Buddhists. The largest monastery was the Navasaṅghārāma. It was situated outside the city in the south-west, and had been built by a former king of the country. The Śāstra masters of this monastery were considered to be the great authorities in the Buddhist world to the north of the Hindukush, and were famous for their original contribution in the interpretation of the Śāstras. The main hall of the convent contained a beautiful image of Buddha. "Within the convent, in the southern hall of Buddha, there is the washing basin which Buddha used. It contains about a peck and is of various colours, which dazzle the eyes. It is difficult to name the gold and stone of which it is made". In the same hall there were, besides other relics,— a tooth of Buddha, his sweeping brush, and a handle ornamented with various gems. These objects were the objects of worship during the fast days. In the neighbourhood of the Navasangharama the pilgrim visited another famous convent which was very old, and frequented by people from distant lands. It was the abode of a large number of people of great talent.

Navasangharama is also known from Arabic sources. It is mentioned under the name Nawbahar, and its high priests were called Paramaka (Barmaka). The monastery was destroyed by the Arabs in the end of the 7th century. Ibn al-Faqih, who wrote in the beginning of the 10th century, tells us that the temple belonged to the idolaters (Buddhists), who held the same faith as the Chinese emperors and the Kabul-Shah. We are further told that many pilgrims used to come here to pay reverence to the largest of the idols. The administration of the Nawbahar was in the hands of the Barmakid family, who governed an estate of 8 farsakhs in length and 4 in width. After the destruction of the monastery, the Barmakids were converted to Islam and went to Baghdad where, as ministers of Harun al-Rashid, they exercised great influence on the cultural life of the capital. They were responsible for sending ambassadors to India in search of Sanskrit books of Astronomy and Mathematics and Medicine, and these books were translated into Arabic under their supervision. These translations gave an impetus to the scientific investigation in the Arab world.

At the time of Hiuan-tsang Tokharestan was under Turkish rule. Kunduz was then a temporary residence of the Turkish chief. The Turkish Kagan had already imbibed some interest in Buddhism before the arrival of the pilgrim. This interest had been created through the efforts of an Indian Buddhist scholar of Nalanda — Prabhakaramitra. Prabhakaramitra was one of the most famous professors of Nalanda who came to the court of the Kagan with 10 disciples, most probably about 620 A. D. He was well received by the Turkish chief, and so long as he was with the Kagan he continued to teach him the Buddhist religion. It was with the permission of the Kagan that he left for China in 626. The eldest son of the Kagan, who had his court at Kunduz, had married the daughter of the king of Kao-ch'ang (Turfan), and some Buddhist influence was also exerted through this princess. In fact, Hiuan-tsang was well received by him, as he possessed a letter of recommendation from the king of Turfan.

Kunduz had become a sort of centre of Buddhist learning at that time. Hiuan-tsang met there a famous Buddhist teacher named Ta-mo-seng-kia (Dharmasinha). He had formerly gone to India for education, and to the north of the Hindukush. The Buddhists of different countries considered him an authority, a *fa-tsiang* (law-maker). He was held in great esteem by the Buddhists of Khotan and Kashgar. He was an excellent scholar of the Vibhasa, and Hiuan-tsang had a discussion with him.

IRAN AND SOGDIANA

Parthian relations with India, as is well known, are very old and go back to the Achamenian period. Parthian satrapies had also been established in North-Western India already before the Christian era, but these did not probably result in the inflow of Buddhist culture to Iran proper. Real interest in Buddhism is shown by Parthians only after the establishment of Buddhism in Tokharestan under the Kushans. The Tokharians must have transmitted Buddhism to them. Although we do not find any remains of old Parthian translations of Buddhist texts, we know from Chinese accounts that a number of Iranian Buddhist scholars had gone to China in the 2nd and 3rd centuries A. D. and collaborated in the translation of Buddhist texts into Chinese. As there was no centre of Buddhist studies in Iran proper, it seems that the Parthian monks had studied Buddhism and the original Buddhist texts in the Buddhist centres of Tokharestan, for example in Balkh, before proceeding to China.

The names of Parthian Buddhist monks in Chinese are distinguished by the prefix An (Ngan) from the old Chinese name of Parthia An-she (Arsak), a name given to the country during the rule of the Arsacidan dynasty. It was in the year 148 A. D., at the commencement of the war which brought about the downfall of the Arsacidan dynasty, that a Parthian prince appears in the western frontier country of China with a burden of Buddhist texts. He is known to the Chinese historian as Ngan-She-Kao or Lokottama (?), the Parthian. He was a true prince of royal descent, but abdicated the throne in favour of his uncle, left the family and turned out a Buddhist monk at an early age. He was a scholar of profound intelligence, and gave himself up to Buddhist studies. He left for China and reached Lo-yang in 144 A. D. He settled down there in the monastery of Po-ma-sse "the White Horse Monastery" built for the first two Indian monks, Dharmaratna and Kasyapa Matanga. He soon succeeded in founding a school of translators which came to be known as "Unrivalled." Really it was such. Ngan-She-Kao himself translated into Chinese more than a hundred Buddhist texts of which 55 are still extant. Many of these texts are extracts from the Buddhist Agamas, generally illustrating the fundamental doctrines of Buddhism. Another Parthian named Ngan Hiuan who belonged to this school came to Lo-yang as a merchant. He received the imperial favour for rendering some valuable service to the public, and obtained the title of the "Chief Officer of the Cavalry." But he soon gave up all official distinctions and embraced the Buddhist religion. As a scholar, he collaborated with the monks of the White Horse Monastery and translated a fairly large number of important Buddhist texts into Chinese.

Amongst the workers of the school of Ngan-She-Kao, we find some Sogdian monks and, what is more interesting, a Chinese priest of the end of the 2nd century A. D., the first we have ever heard, named Yen-Fo-t'iao (Buddhadeva). He was a patient collaborator of Ngan Hiuan, learnt Sanskrit (-?, the original language of the sacred texts brought from Central Asia) and was able to recite the whole of the Pratimoksa. He was given the title of Acarya and a Sanskrit name, Buddhadeva (Fo-t'iao). To the same school of Ngan-She-Kao belonged also the famous Indo-Scythian monk, Lokaksema.

It is not without significance that the first organised effort made to translate the Buddhist Canon into Chinese was made by Ngan-She-Kao. Buddhism, as we have already seen, was introduced into China by the Indo-Scythians, and it was through them that China first came to know of India. It was also left to this great Parthian to lay the foundation of a school for a systematic interpretation of Buddhism to the Chinese, and it was in that school that the first Chinese Acarya and Sanskrit scholar received his training.

Parthian monks of minor importance went to China during the 3rd and the 4th centuries A. D. They also contributed not only to the spread of Buddhism in China but also to the work of translation of the Buddhist texts, which was only possible for those who possessed an intimate knowledge of the Indian language in which they were written down.

Ancient Sogdiana was situated to the North of Tokharestan with its centre at Samarcand. The people are mentioned by the Achamenian rulers and the Greeks : Herodotus — under the name Sogdoi, Behistun inscription — Suguda. Avesta — Sughda. The Sogdians and the people of the North-East spoke an Iranian language called Areioi (Haraiva) which was one of the Scythic languages. Herodotus says that the Sogdoi had as neighbours — Xorasmioi (Uvarazmiya, Areioi i. e. Haraiva, Parthoi, Gandarioi, Dadixai — the inscriptions mention : Parthians, Ariena, Sogdians, Xorazmians, Bactrians, Zarankes, Sakas, and Gandarians. According to Strabon, the Scythic language was little different from the languages of the Sogdians, Khorazmians, Ossetes and Alans. In the time of Alexander there was very close relation between the partly nomadic, partly agriculturist nobles, merchants and travellers of Sogdiana and the nomads of the North and North-East —

Massagetai, Sakai and Scuthai. According to the Mahomedan sources, the Persian language was of 7 kinds : Haravi, Sagzi, Zavuli, Sughdi which are lost and Parsi, Dari and Pehlevi which are current. Haravi of Herat (Palh, Harew, Arm. Hrev), Sagistan, Zawulistan and Sughd. Sogdians 'were in close contact with India, where they were known as Śulika. a name derived from Iranian Sughdik—Suwdik. The people and their language have long disappeared, but the remnants of the ancient Sogdian language have been discovered from a few Sogdian translations of Buddhist texts brought from various parts of Eastern Turkestan by archaeologists. As ancient Tokharians (Yue-ches) had once lived in that region before occupying Tokharestan proper, there were many close links between the people of the two regions. Buddhism must have been carried to Sogdiana by the Tokharian monks.

The Sogdians were famous traders, and in course of their trade they had gone to different parts of Central Asia and established colonies. At the beginning of the Christian era these colonies were fairly numerous and there was almost a Sogdian route from Samarcand up to the Chinese wall. They had come in contact with Buddhist culture in other parts of Central Asia as well in later times.

Sogdian monks had played some part in the transmission of Buddhist culture to China. Their names are distinguished in Chinese by the prefix K'ang, the ancient name of Sogdiana in Chinese being K'ang-kiu. We have already seen that some of these Sogdian monks had collaborated with Ngan She-Kao. A very illustrious Sogdian monk worked in South China in the 3rd century. He was Seng hui (Sanghamati ?).

Seng-hui was born of a Sogdian family. His ancestors at first settled down in India. His father was a merchant, and had to stay in Tonkin (Kiao-che). Seng-hui was born there in the first quarter of the 3rd century A. D. On the death of his father, he left the world and became a monk. He soon proceeded to Nanking, where he built a monastery and founded a Buddhist school. He was the first to introduce Buddhism in Southern China. There is some truth in it. Cche Kien, the Indo-Scythian, who was translating Buddhist texts in Nanking at about the same time, was only an Upasaka, a layman. So he had no right to give ordination to the novice. Seng-hui was a perfect monk, and had exercised his full rights by converting many Chinese to the new faith which he had brought to them. Seng-hui translated about a dozen Buddhist texts into Chinese, and some of them have come down to us.

ANCIENT BUDDHIST SITES

Archaeological work in Tokharestan is still in an exploratory stage. Various sites have been spotted out, but no systematic work has been done either on the Russian side or on the Afghan side. The remains of ancient art that have been discovered in Bamiyan, which was included within the sphere of Tokharian influence and which we have already discussed, clearly show that at least in the territories on this side of the Oxus, and specially in Balkh, Buddhist art must have been in a very flourishing state in ancient times.

The explorations carried on in various parts of Tokharestan have led to the discovery of very important finds and location of interesting sites. The site of the ancient city of Balkh has been examined on many occasions. But unfortunately nothing has been discovered on the surface. Only excavations of the sites can yield results. Balkh was a prosperous seat of Buddhism, and as late as the time of Hiuan-tsang its monasteries were living centres of the faith. The Navasangharama, we have seen, contained beautiful images of Buddha. Balkh suffered most from foreign invasions. It was first destroyed by the Arabs towards the end of the 7th century soon after the departure of Hiuan-tsang. The Arabs first built a new town in the locality of Baryqan, 2 farsakhs from Balkh. In 725 Governor Abdullah restored the town on the former site, and the representatives of the Barmakid family were entrusted with the work of rebuilding. In 870 it was again partially destroyed by Yaqub of the Saffavid dynasty. In the Tahirid and the Samanid period, Balkh again rose to be one of the largest cities equal to Merv or Herat. The hordes of Chingiz Khan destroyed it again so totally that in the 14th century, when Ibn Batutta visited the place, it was still in ruins. The ruins extended over an area of 16 miles.

But in other sites of Tokharestan, which were not so much affected by the foreign invasions, remains of Buddhist art have been discovered even on the surface. Thus in Haibak, which is situated on the Khulm river, a monolithic stupa has been discovered. It is of the type of Kailasa temple of Ellora. The initiative must have been of Indian origin. The stupa is incomplete in certain places, and that must have been due to the Hephthalite invasion of the 5th century. There was also a Sangharama attached to the stupa, and its remains are also visible. The ruins of Haibak form the connecting link between Balkh and Bamiyan.

The next group of interesting ruins have been discovered at Kunduz. Remains of Graeco-Buddhist art, and also art-remains which reveal direct Indian influence of the 4th-5th centuries, have been found in the neighbourhood of Kunduz.

Termez, as may be supposed from the account of Hiuan-tsang, was also an important centre of Buddhism. This city suffered considerably in the hands of the invaders. It was first conquered by the Arabs in 704. The ancient town on the river bank was destroyed by Chingiz Khan. Old coins, majority of which belong to the Greek period, have been discovered from the ruins of the old city. Coins of Kanishka and Huvishka also have been found. Abundant ruins affiliated to Graeco-Buddhist art have also been discovered. An important stupa, the Kata-Stupa, is of the type found in Gandhara. Images of Bodhisattvas of the type found in Kucha and Taxila have also been found on the site.

CHAPTER III

EASTERN TURKESTAN — THE SOUTHERN STATES

FROM THE PAMIR TO KASHGAR

The southern states of the Tarim basin may be divided into three groups according to the zones of cultural influences : (i) Kashgar and the neighbouring states, (ii) Khotan and the neighbouring states and (iii) the region of Lobnor. While speaking of the Pamir states we have already pointed out that two of these States to the East of Shughnan viz. Kie-pan-to (Sarikol) and Wu-sha (Yangi Hissar) culturally belonged to Kashgar. Hiuan-tsang tells us that in his times the spoken and written languages of Kie-pan-to, Wu-sha and Kashgar were the same. As the writing in Kashgar is said to have been of Indian origin, based on the Brahmi, we may suppose that the same writing was current in the two other states.

Of the Chinese travellers, Song-yun is the first to mention Sarikol under the name Ho-pan-to, which he visited on his way from Khotan to India. Hiuan-tsang, we have seen, mentions it under the name Kie-pan-to. The T'ang Annals mention it under various names : Ho-pan-to, Han-to, Ko-kuan-t'o etc. Hiuan-tsang tells us that the capital of the state was backed by the river Sita, (Hsi-to) which is now identified with the Yarkand Darya. This ancient capital has been located at modern Tashkurghan, which contains ruins of very early times.

Buddhism was quite prosperous in this small state in the middle of the 7th century. In that period there were more than 10 monasteries in the capital with 500 monks, all followers of the Sarvastivada school. The reigning king then was a patron of Buddhism and a scholar of great culture. He belonged to a very old dynasty, claiming origin from the 'Solar Race' and had probably the title of Devaputra, a title of Chinese origin used for the first time by the Kushan emperors of India. The dynasty may have had some connection with the Kushans, as one of its early rulers tried to emulate the example of Kanishka by patronising Buddhist scholars of India.

The story is told by Hiuan-tsang. A famous Buddhist scholar of

Taksasila, Kumaralata, was brought by force by the king of the country from India to live and teach in his country. Kumaralata was the founder of the Sautrantika school of Buddhism and was according to tradition, a contemporary of Asvaghosa, Nagarjuna and Aryadeva. He thus lived in the 3rd century and was probably a younger contemporary of Kanishka. He is said to have written many treatises, but so far only one book, the *Kalpanāmaṇḍitikā*, which again is the recast of the *Sutrālaṁkāra* of Asvaghosa, has been partially discovered from Eastern Turkestan. The monastery built for Kumaralata by the local king could still be seen in the 7th century. The fame of Kumaralata had spread to Tokharestan and Eastern Turkestan, and this explains the reason why this solitary manuscript bearing his name could be discovered only in Eastern Turkestan.

The next country on the way to Kashgar was Wu-sha. Its southern boundary is given as the Sita or the Yarkand river. It was situated on the eastern slopes of the Tsung-ling (Pamirs). In the time of Hiuan-tsang there were in this country more than 10 monasteries with nearly 1000 monks of the Sarvastivada school. The country has been identified with Yangi-Hissar in the extreme North-West of the Yarkand oasis.

Kashgar, the most important state in this area, played a significant role in ancient times, as it does now in the transmission of culture to the northern and southern states of the Tarim basin. It was situated at the junction of two routes, one leading towards South-East i. e. Khotan region, and the other towards the North-East i. e. the Kucha region. Kashgar has been mentioned in the Chinese sources under varying names: In the Dynastic Annals from the Han to the T'ang times the name is given as Shu-lei of which a variant Sha-lei is given by Song-yun, Kumarajiva, Fa-yong (beginning of the 5th century), Dharmagupta (end of the 6th cent.) and Wu-k'ong (middle of the 8th cent.). Hiuan-tsang and some of his contemporary authors mention it as K'ia-sha of which variants are found as Kia-she and Ki-sha. Fa-hien alone gives another form of the name as Kie-ch'a.

A Chinese Buddhist text of a very late period would explain the name Shu-le as an abbreviation of K'ia-lu-shu-tan-le i. e.,

Kharoṣṭra, but for want of confirmation this explanation has been considered fanciful. In a Sanskrit-Chinese Dictionary of the 7th century, another Chinese name of Kashgar is given as 'Hu'—'Barbarian" but its local name is mentioned as Suri (or Suli). The ancient Chinese Shu-lei or Su-li also was based on a local name like Surik or Sulik. But the country was known more commonly under the name K'ia-sha which is supposed to have been based on Khaśa. Although there are difficulties in accepting this identification, it cannot be denied that the people of the locality were known in India as Khaśa or Khaśya. Their script is mentioned in the Lalitavistara as Khaśyalipi. It has been suggested that the same country is mentioned in Ptolemy's geography as *Kasia ori*. It is only after the Muslim conquest that the present name Kashgar or Qashqar came in use. The Tibetans used to call the country Ga-'jag which probably is preserved in the old Niya documents as Kaṁjaka. In some Tibetan texts also this name is found as Kañcaki.

According to Han Annals, the Sai or the Saka people before their defeat in the hands of the Great Yue-ches were settled in Tokharestan. It was in that period that Su-le (Kashgar) and all other kingdoms to its North-West belonged to the Saka people. In the first century B. C. Kashgar became a Chinese protectorate. Later on it was conquered by the rulers of Khotan, who were probably allies of the Kushans. Kashgar was reconquered by the Chinese under Pan-chao towards the end of the 1st century A. D. The country was soon after conquered by the Kushans (Yue-ches) in the beginning of the 2nd century when An-kuo ruler of Kashgar was obliged to send hostages to the Kushan emperor. Between 114 and 120 the Kushan emperor deposed the successor of An-kuo and placed Ch'en-p'an on the throne. It is likely that the hostages sent by China to Kanishka as mentioned by Hiuan-tsang were no other than these hostages of the ruler of Kashgar. These hostages used to live in the Punjab in winter but were allowed to go to Kapiśa for their summer residence. The monastery in Kapiśa built for them was called Sha-lo-kia or Saraka which probably was an echo of Sha-lei or Sarak, the ancient name of Kashgar.

We do not hear anything about Kashgar during the subsequent centuries when probably it was part of the Khotanese kingdom. It is only in the period 452-466 A. D., we hear of an embassy being sent to the Chinese court by the King of Kashgar to present a Buddhist sacred relic and an old dress of Buddha which could not be burnt. In the beginning of the 6th century Kashgar was under the Hephthalite rule. The Hepthalite empire was destroyed by the Turks between 563 and 567, and all the states which were formerly under the Hephthalite rule accepted the suzerainty of the Turks. But as in the case of other states, Kashgar also was allowed to retain its local autonomy.

With the establishment of the T'ang dynasty in China in 618 the Chinese tried to reconquer the Tarim basin and the disruption in the Turkish empire soon facilitated their task. Western Turks were completely defeated in 658 and the Chinese re-established their suzerainty in Eastern Turkestan. The whole of this region was divided into four administrative divisions called "Four Garrisons" and Kashgar with states in its immediate neighbourhood formed one of these Garrisons. The Chinese, however, lost the whole of the Eastern Turkestan within a century. Tibetans started a long drawn war against the Chinese in 662, specially in the Eastern part of the Tarim basin. The Arabs joined the fray in the beginning of the 8th century and these led to a complete defeat of the Chinese army in 751. The Chinese control of certain areas continued for some years, but since 791 all the territories were lost to the Chinese.

We know something about the local history of Kashgar from the T'ang Annals. The name of the ruling family in the T'ang period was P'ei. The chief of Kashgar in 728, P'ei Ngan-che had this title. In 753 the ambassador who went to China from Kashgar had the name P'ei Kuo-liang. The ruler of Kashgar in 786, when Wu-k'ong visited the country, was P'ei Leng-leng. The rulers were also called A-mo-che (*amacca*), a title which was also borne by the rulers of Khotan in this period.

We have seen that Indian writing was current in Kashgar. It was in all likelihood the Brahmi in its slanting form that is found in the old documents from different parts of the Tarim basin. Kharosthi was current in some parts of Khotan up to the 3rd century and that was probably the script known in Kashgar in the early period. Brahmi was introduced in the 4th-5th centuries when Kharosthi went out of use.

We do not have much definite information on the language of ancient Kashgar. In all likelihood it was a dialect of Eastern Iranian, the ancient Khotanese being another dialect. The Eastern Iranian is often described as Saka language. The language of Kashgar, however, must have undergone a deep Indian influence through Buddhism. We have just seen that the title of the king was A-mo-che (*amacca* which is to be derived from Sanskrit amātya, Pkt. *amacca*). A few other words quoted in Chinese documents point to the same direction. We are told that the Sanskrit word Upādhyāya meaning teacher had the form Wu-she = 'uo-dz'i = *ojhā* in Kashgar and Ho-shang = ua-'ziang = *ujhā* in Khotan.

Fa-hien, who visited the country towards the closing years of the 4th century, found Buddhism in a very prosperous condition. Amongst the various Buddhist relics, he found there the spitoon, alms-bowl and the tooth of Buddha preserved in a stupa. In his times there were in Kashgar more than two thousand monks with their disciples, all followers of Hinayana, probably of the Sarvastivada school. They were strict followers of the Buddhist discipline. During his stay in the capital, the pilgrim also witnessed the quin-quennial assembly (pañcavārṣika) convoked by the king. Monks from all quarters had been invited to the assembly and it was a grand spectacle. For nearly seven days the king and his ministers made special offerings and gifts to the assembled monks. Other Chinese pilgrims, Che-mong (404), Fa-yong and Tao-yo (420), who visited the country soon after, also testify to what Fa-hien says.

Hiuan-tsang gives a more detailed description of the condition of Buddhism in the country. He found that the people were sincere followers of Buddhism, and honestly practised the rules of discipline. There were several hundreds of monasteries with nearly 10000 monks, all followers of the Sarvastivada school

Many of them could recite the Buddhist texts, and even the entire Tripitaka and the Vibhasa. This literature was in Sanskrit and it is evident that Sanskrit was seriously cultivated by the local Buddhist scholars. The last Chinese pilgrim to pass through Kashgar was Wu-k'ong, who travelled back to China about 786.

Indian scholars used frequently to go to Kashgar. Kumarajiva, who was born in Kucha of an Indian father and a Kuchean mother, had gone to Kashmir for his education during the last decade of the 4th century. On his way back from Kashmir he came to Kashgar and stayed there for nearly a year. He worshipped there the alms-bowl of Buddha and studied the Abhidharma of the Sarvastivada school with its six pādas or divisions of this literature. This shows that there were very competent teachers of the Abhidharma there to help him in his studies. A master of Tripitaka named Hi-kien requested the king to retain Kumarajiva permanently in Kashgar, but this could not be done as the king of Kucha was pressing him to return to Kucha. But before leaving the place Kumarajiva further studied the four Vedas, the five sciences, the Brahmanical Śāstras and also astronomy at Kashgar. If this account is true then we must believe that Kashgar was some sort of centre of Brahmanical studies too. During his stay there, two great personalities came to Kumarajiva for ordination. They were Suryabhadra and Suryasoma who were the two sons of the king of So-kiu (Karghalik-Yarkand). They were followers of Mahayana. Kumarajiva taught them *Śataśāstra* and *Mādhyamikaśāstra* before taking the route for Kucha.

A few years earlier a great Indian scholar, Buddhayasas of Kashmir had come to Kashgar. This Buddhayasas was of great help to Kumarajiva in his studies at Kashgar. The two became great friends. Buddhayasas stayed in Kashgar after the departure of Kumarajiva and continued to exercise a great influence on the local king. The king first met him in an assembly of 3000 monks (probably the pañcavārṣika assembly). The king's name is given as Pu-t'u (* pu't-d'uo — *Vardha ?). The king's son Ta-mo-fo-to (Dharmaputra) was much impressed by the friendly manners of

Dharmayasas, and on knowing that he was an Indian, invited him to stay in the palace. Kucha was invaded by the Chinese in 382. Being anxious about the safety of Kumarajiva, Buddhayasas induced the king of Kashgar to send an army to the help of Kucha. An army was really sent under the leadership of the prince and Buddhayasas accompanied him as adviser. But Kucha fell to the Chinese before the army could reach there. Buddhayasas ultimately joined Kumarajiva in China where they worked together. So great was the personal bond between the two.

Almost towards the close of the Buddhist period another Indian scholar Dharmacandra was found in Kashgar. He was a Buddhist monk of Magadha and had gone to China in 730 from Kucha on the invitation of the Chinese ambassador. On the completion of his work in China be started in 741 on his return journey to India He passed through different countries ultimately reaching Kashgar. From Kashgar he went to Shughnan but on account of political unrest in that area he had to go back to Kashgar. As it was then impossible to pass to India, he ultimately settled in Khotan where he died in 743.

A number of old Buddhist stupas are still found in various sites around Kashgar, although other antiquities are very scarce.

The route from Kashgar towards the South-East across the Sita river (Yarkand Darya) led towards the ancient country of Che-kiu-kia. It was a part of the kingdom of Khotan and culturally too, it was under the domination of that country. Hiuan-tsang tells us clearly that the writing used there was like that of Khotan, although the language was slightly different. The name of the country is given in the Chinese sources under different forms : Tsu-ku, So-kiu, Che-kiu-kia, etc. The T'ang Annals say that the ancient name of the country under the Han was Tseu-ho. The Tibetan texts give the name as Cu-gu-pan, thus agreeing with the T'ang Annals which give the alternative names of Che-kiu-kia as Chu-ku-po or Chu-ku-pan. The earlier Chinese names Tseu-ho (* dz'i-go-), Tsu-ku (*tsiwo-gu), So-kiu. Che-kiu-kia all point to an original like Cogu or Coguga. This name is found under the form Cokkuka from the Central Asian documents. The other Chinese name might have been Coguva, but this evidently came in vogue long after the time of Hiuan-tsang. Cokkuka has been identified with Karghahalik-Yarkand.

About the condition of Buddhism in Cokkuka, Hiuan-tsang tells us that the people were sincere Buddhists, enjoyed good works and that the country possessed some tens of monasteries with more than 100 monks, all followers of Mahayana. The Mahayana tradition was probably continuous in the country since the 4th century. We have seen that two princes of Cokkuka, Suryabhadra and Suryasoma had gone to Kashgar towards the end of the 4th century to receive initiation from Kumarajiva and to study Mahayana texts with him. As the names of the princes indicate, probably a ruling dynasty of Indian origin had been established in Cokkuka very early.

KHOTAN — ANCIENT TRADITION

Information on Khotan and its adjoining states is plentiful in various sources, Chinese, Tibetan and archaeological. The ancient names of the country occur in these sources under different forms : Yu-t'ien (the oldest form), Yu-tun, K'iu-tan, Huo-tan etc. All these forms go back to an original like Godana or Khotana. Another Chinese name which was probably more learned was K'iu-sa-ta-na i. e. Kustana. Old Kharosthi documents of the Khotan region which belong to the third century mention the names under the forms Kustana, Khotana, Khodana, and Khodamna. The most ancient name probably was Godāna which is found in the Buddhist literature as a northern continent. The Tibetan sources commonly mention the country under the name Li-yul or the country of Li and its capital as U-then. The name Li is not found in any other source. It may have been preserved in Ilchi which is the name of modern Khotan.

The ancient Annals of Khotan have been preserved in various recensions in Tibetan translations. The originals had been compiled in all appearance in Sanskrit. It gives a traditional account of the country for nearly 1256 years from the foundation of the kingdom till the time of the destruction of Buddhism, in Khotan. The foundation of the kingdom is attributed to a son of Asoka. It is said that Asoka, while in course of pilgrimage came to Khotan in search of sacred sites. At this time the King's chief consort gave birth to a boy. The soothsayers predicated that the boy would be king before the death of his father. The king thought that it indicated a bad omen and abandoned the child there. The child was nourished by the mother-earth and thus came to be known as Earth-Breast "Ku-stana." The child was eventually adopted by the great king of China (Ts'in She Huang-ti). The boy, when grown up, quarrelled with the king and with a force of 10000 men came to Khotan in a search of land.

About the same time Yasa, the minister of Asoka fell in disgrace of the king and left the country with 7000 followers, ultimately reaching Khotan in search of new lands. After some clashes between the followers of Yasa and those of Kustana both came to an agreement through divine intervention. A kingdom was founded with Kustana as its king and Yasa as his minister. The western part of the country to the West of the Khotan river was organised by the Chinese, whereas the eastern portion was organised by the Indians. The land between the rivers was organised by the Chinese and the Indians jointly. Thus Khotan became the country where the Chinese and the Indians met.

The new kingdom thus consisted of three parts : the Chinese zone which we are told included two provinces : Kon-sed and Ku-sed, the intermediate zone between the two rivers which was under joint occupation and the Indian zone in the East which was called Skam-sed. Thus it seems that the Chinese came from the Kashgar side while the Indians from the East through the Kara-korum passes.

We are told that the kingdom of Khotan was founded 234 years after Nirvana i. e. about 240 B. C. The Annals give the names of rulers of 56 generations. The grandson of Kustana was named Vijayasambhava and since then all successive rulers had the names beginning with Vijaya, such as Vijaya-virya,-jaya,-dharma,-simha,-kirti,-samgrama,-bala,-vikrama and so on. The Annals also speak of the Buddhist foundations attributed to various rulers of the country.

Buddhism was first introduced in Khotan during the reign of

King Vijayasambhava who was the grandson of Kustana. The Annals say that the monk Arya Vairocana who was an incarnation of Maitreya on coming to Khotan settled in the grove called Tsu-le (Cu-le) in the province of Tsar-ma. Here he met the king and became his pious friend (Kalyanamitra). Vijayasambhava built for Vairocana the great monastery of Tsar-ma, which was the first in Khotan. Vairocana was also responsible for bringing miraculously the relics of Buddha from Kashmir. This story is also told by Song-yun and Hiuan-tsang in details. They besides give the additional information- that Vairocana had gone from Kashmir. The date of this first foundation, according to the Tibetan Annals, would be about 211 B. C. The Chinese sources tell us that the monastery had a stupa which was called "the stupa of up-turned bowl." This was because Vairocana told the king at the time of building the monastery that the stupa should have the shape of an up-turned bowl. Song-yun mentions the name of the monastery as Tsan-mo which is the same as Tsarma of the Tibetan sources. Sir Aurel Stein has conclusively identified the old site of Tsarma with Chalma-kazan in the neighbourhood of Yotkan. The name of the place was Chalma (*Charma). Kazan means pot or bowl. Thus the modern name preserves the old tradition. Discovery of a number of antiquities, terra-cotta, broken images etc. confirmed the antiquity of the site.

The Tibetan Annals speak of the foundation of a number of other monasteries during the reigns of subsequent rulers. About eight generations after the foundation of the Tsarma convent three Arhats : Buddhaduta, Khagata and Khagadrod went from India and settled at Aryastana (-sthāna) of Hge'u-to-san. King Vijayavirya built two monasteries for them : one was the Hgum-tir (Gomati) and the other was the Hge'u-to-san on the Gośīrṣa hill. Three generations later the Chinese princess, Punesvar, who was the queen of King Vijayajaya and responsible for introducing seri-culture in Khotan, built two monasteries—Potarya and Maza for the sake of her Kalyanamitra Arya Samghaghosa who had gone from India. The king had three sons ; the eldest Dharmananda became a monk, and went to India. He was a follower of the Mahasanghika school and built eight monasteries of Hdro-tir and eight of Kam-sed, all of which belonged to this sect. Number of monasteries increased during subsequent generations and towards the close of the Buddhist period the number according to the Tibetan Annals stood thus : "Inside the fort and outside there are 68. To be classed as medium monasteries are 95. To be classed as small monasteries are 148. Of minor chapels—there are—3,688......" The number of such monasteries in the neighbouring places was also high.

Hiuan-tsang speaks in detail about the condition of Buddhism in Khotan. According to him, there were in the capital over 100 monasteries with 5000 monks. They were all followers of Mahayana. The pilgrim also mentions some of the principal monasteries. Besides the oldest one of Tsarma, there were the monasteries of Ti-ko-p'o-fa-na, Sha-mo-no, Gośṛnga and Mo-she. Ti-ko-p'o-fa-na (Dirghabhavana ?) was built to contain an image of Buddha which had miraculously come to Khotan. This was probably the same as Bha-va-na of Hgum-tir mentioned by the Tibetan Annals and located by Stein at Bowa-Kambar. The monastery of Sha-mo-no or Sha-mo-jo is said to have been an important convent with a stupa nearly 100 feet high. This seems to be the Sum-na of the Tibetan text which was built by King Vijayasimha for Anandasena, the king of Kashgar who became a Buddhist after his defeat at the hands of the Khotan king. The ruins have been located at the village of Somiya in the neighbourhood of Yotkan. The monastery of Mo-she built by the Chinese queen of a former king (Vijayajaya of the Tibetan text) was surely the same as Maza built in commemoration of successful introduction of seri-culture. Its ruins have been located at Kum-i-Shahidan.

The most important centre of Buddhist culture was the monasteries of Gomati (Hgum-tir) and Gośīrṣa or Gośṛṅga. The Gomati monastery is described by Fa-hien in details. "Attached to it", he says, there were "three thousand monks, who are called to their meals by the sound of a bell. When they enter the refectory their demeanour is marked by a reverent gravity, and they take their seats in regular order, all maintaining a perfect silence. No sound is heard from their alms-bowls and other utensils. When any of these pure men require food they are not allowed to call out for it but only make signs with their hands". The monks of this monastery in his time were all followers of Mahayana and were held in high esteem by the king.

The Gośṛṅga or Gośīrṣa monastery was built later on the slopes of the Gośṛṅga mountain. It was supposed to be a spot formerly visited by Buddha. The inmates were all Mahayanists in the time of Hiuan-tsang. The monastery is also mentioned in the *Sūryagarbha-sūtra*, a Buddhist canonical text which was translated into Chinese between 589 and 619. The stupa is called 'the Caitya of the Saint Gomasala-Gandha' (Kiu-mo-so-lo hsiang) situated on the mount Gośīrṣa on the steep bank of the Khotan river. The site has been located in the Kohmari hill on the bank of the Kara-Kash. There is a two-storied cave on the spot to mark the ancient site. This is the place where a manuscript of very far-reaching importance was discovered. This was the fragmentary manuscript of Prakrit *Dharmapada* in Kharosthi writing which was procured by the French explorer Dutreuil de Rhins in 1890.

HISTORICAL ACCOUNTS

The information which we get from the Chinese Annals on the history of Khotan more or less confirm the Tibetan account. A local dynasty, which had the title of Vijaya, had been ruling in Khotan since very early times, and it was left undisturbed by the Chinese after their periodic conquests and establishment of suzerainty over the Khotanese territories. This dynasty was certainly of Indian origin, as is clearly shown by the names of its members. Hiuan-tsang tells us emphatically that from the time of the foundation of Khotan till his days the succession of rulers of the same dynasty had been in regular order, and the power had been lineally transmitted.

Embassy from Khotan was sent to China for the first time under Emperor Wu-ti (140-87 B. C.). Khotan in this period was a small state with a population of 19,300. The other small states in its neighbourhood were independent in this period. The Chinese Annals say that during the second quarter of the

1st century A. D. Khotan became subject to the kingdom of So-k'iu (Cokkuka), but soon after, during the period 58-73 A. D., a Khotanese general named Hsiu-mo-pa revolted and asserted the independence of Khotan. His nephew and successor Kuang-te conquered Cokkuka, and Khotan soon became so powerful that all the states in the North-West up to Kashgar submitted to her. The Tibetan Annals also refer to this war, but not with Cokkuka but with Kashgar. During the reign of king Vijaya-siṁha, 16th in descent from Kustana, Khotan is said to have been invaded by the king of Ga-'jag (Kashgar). The king was however defeated, taken prisoner and subsequently released. On his return to Kashgar, the king became a Buddhist monk and later on retired to a monastery in Khotan. He was given the name of Anandasena by the king of Khotan. The king called Kuan-te in the Chinese sources seems to have been the same as Vijaya-simha. The same king played some part during the invasion of Pan-ch'ao in 73 A. D. He allied himself with Pan-ch'ao, fought against the Huns, and ultimately accepted the Chinese suzerainty. The Chinese hold on Khotan soon became weak, and the Kushans under Kanishka established their political supremacy at least in the western part of the Tarim basin. In fact, the Tibetan Annals tells us that the successor of Vijayasimha allied himself with King Kanika of Guzan (Kanishka of Kushan) and helped him in his conquest of Eastern India as far as Soked (Sāketa).

In 129 A. D. Fang-Kien, king of Khotan, killed the ruler of Yu-mi (also called Kiu-mi—Keriya) and gave the territory to his own son. In 151-152 Ch'eng-kuo, who was a relative of the ancient king of Yu-mi reported against Kien to the Chinese court and killed Kien in a treacherous attack. This led to a revolt in Khotan under the leadership of the local Governor Shu-p'o against the Chinese. The Chinese commander was killed and Ngan-kuo the son of Kien succeeded to the throne. The Chinese, however, did not attempt at a retaliation. Khotan sent embassies to China between 202 and 220. With the fall of the Han dynasty in China Khotan became still stronger and subjugated the neighbouring territories of Yu-mi (Keriya), Su-le (Kashgar) and Yung-lu during the period 220-264. Khotan sent another embassy to China in 222.

In 445 Khotan was invaded by Mu-li-yen, the chief of the Tu-yuk-hun. The king of Khotan was killed and the country was ravaged. This account is also given in the Tibetan Annals, which mention the Tu-yuk-hun under the name of Drug-gu. During the reign of king Vijayasamgrama, Khotan was invaded by A-no-so, the Drug-gu chief, monasteries as far as Hg'eu-to-san were burnt, and the country was devastated. Vijaya-samgrama was then minor. It is said that when he attained age he retaliated against the Tu-yuk-hun in the same manner. In any way, Khotan must have recovered very soon, and normal embassies were sent to China a number of times between 542 and 541, although Khotan had to accept the nominal suzerainty of the Hephthalites in this period.

Under the Sui (581-618), the king of Khotan was Wang and his title Pei-she-pi-lien (Vijaya-). The T'ang Annals also tell us that the family of the ruling dynasty of Khotan was called Wei-ch'e (Vijaya). The same Annals also mention the names of some of the kings of Khotan and all of them had this title of Vijaya. The personal name of the king who sent an embassy to China in 632 and his son in 635 to be enrolled in the Imperial guard was Wu-mi. In 643-649 the king of Khotan was Fu-tu-Sin, who went to China to receive a mandate personally from the Emperor. During the period 674 — 675, the king Fu-tu Hiong went to China with his son, younger brothers and high officials to pay homage to the emperor. The successor of Fu-tu Hiong was Fu-tu King. The successor of Fu-tu-King was Fu-she Chan (Vijaya Fu-she), who was succeeded by Fu-tu Ta. Ta was succeeded by Fu-tu Koei. The successor of Koei, Fu-tu Sheng, went to the help of China in 756-757 with his army. Sheng died in China while his brother Vijaya Yao was ruling the country. Yao was on the throne till 786 when Wu-k'ong visited the country. The Chinese supremacy in Khotan ended about 791. Chinese contact with Khotan in the subsequent period was not very frequent. We hear of a Khotanese king Li Sheng-t'ien, who sent several missions to China from 940 to 966. Buddhist

Khotan resisted long against the Arab invaders, but ultimately succumbed towards the end of the century. By the year 1000 Muslim rule was an accomplished fact in Khotan.

Khotan in the height of her power extended upto Ni-jang (present Niya site) in the east and to So-kiu (Cokkuka) in the west. It comprised originally the five states Jong-lu, Yu-mi, K'iu-le, Pi-shan and Yu-t'ien (Khotan) proper. Later history mentions six, including Khotan proper—Ilchi, present Khotan, Yurung Kash, Kara Kash, Chira, Keriya, Lo-lasung. In the East it included Pi-mo and Ni-jang. Archaeological discoveries made in Khotan and ancient sites to its east have thrown considerable light on the history of ancient Khotan. The explorations have first of all led to the identification of the ancient capital of the country. According to the Chinese accounts, it was situated between the Yurung-kash and Karakash rivers. The Gośṛṅga monastery was only 20 li to the south-west of the city. This shows that the site of the ancient capital is to be located at the village of Yotkan. A constant supply of antiques from this site confirms the identification. The most important finds consisted of a hoard of Sino-Kharosthi coins, which were issued most probably after 74 A. D., when Khotan passed under effective Chinese supremacy. The coins are of "bare horse" and "Bactrian camel" types and thus show some special connections between Khotan rulers and Śaka rulers of India, Maues, Azes and their successors (50 B. C.-80 A. D.). The Kharosthi in the legends closely agree with Indian Kharosthi of the Kushan period. The occurrence of legends both in Chinese and Kharosthi show that they were intended for both the Chinese and the Indian subjects. The royal names occurring in the legends are : Gugramada, Gugradama, Gugramaya, Gugramoda, and Gugratida. If it could be shown that Gugra was a local word meaning "Vijaya", then some connection could be established between this line of kings and the line of the Vijaya kings. Kushan coins of Kujula Kara Kadphises and Kanishka have also been discovered in Yotkan. There are, besides, Chinese coins of all dynasties from the beginning of the 1st century to the end of the 11th. Yotkan has also produced among other antiquities miniature stone carvings and small well-carved Buddhist reliefs of the Gandhara school, which must have been brought from Gandhara region. All these antiquities show that Yotkan had risen to be an active capital city already before the Christian era, and continued to be so till the end of the Buddhist period (11th cent.).

A number of old Buddhist sites excavated in the desert at Dandan Uiliq have brought to light very important finds. Dandan Uiliq was probably the site of ancient Chinese Li-hsie, which was the Chinese garrison headquarters till the end of the 8th century, when it was abandoned by the Chinese. A great abundance of stucco images and relics have been discovered from various sites of Dandan Uiliq. Besides, frescoes with Brahmi inscriptions also have been found. Manuscripts and other records discovered are mostly in Brahmi and Chinese. Brahmi manuscripts have produced fragments of two canonical works of Mahayana—the *Prajñāpāramitā* and *Vajracchedikā* in Sanskrit. Brahmi records in non-Sanskritic languages are mostly in ancient Khotanese, which was an Eastern Iranian language. The Chinese documents are largely official records of the garrison officers of Li-hsie. There are also deeds of private transactions in Chinese. There is also a Judaeo-Persian document, which is a letter from Ispahbud of Tabaristan to Yazid dated about 718 A. D. Buddhist finds similar to those of Dandan Uiliq have also been discovered from ruins of two stupas at a place named Rawak only 7 miles to the north of Danadan Uiliq. The Buddhist images in all these mostly belong to the Gandhara school.

Two very ancient places to the east of Khotan mentioned by Hiuan-tsang were P'i-mo and Ni-jang. At Pi-mo, he witnessed a sandal wood image of Buddha of legendary antiquity as it was supposed to have been made by King Udayana of Kosambi in the life-time of Buddha. The image had miraculously come from another city named O-lao-lo-ka to the north of Khotan, which had been covered by desert sands on account of the sin of the local people. Pi-mo is mentioned as Han-mo by Song-yun. It is Pein of Marco Polo in the region of Chira and Domoko. Ruins of old Buddhist stupas have been found at the old site.

Niya was also a very important Buddhist centre in the time of

Hiuan-tsang, but its more ancient parts were probably destroyed by the erosion of the desert in his times. Explorations in these old sites by Sir Aurel Stein have brought to light finds of very far-reaching importance. A very large number of Kharosthi documents, mostly tablets on wood, has been unearthed from this place. The Kharosthi script is of the 3rd century, and the language of the documents is a Prakrit allied to the Prakrit used in the North-Western frontier of India in the Kushan period. They are mostly official documents starting with the formula : *mahanuava maharaya lihati.* There are also Chinese documents on bamboo slips. The ruins of stupas, residential houses, arbour, orchards, lanes etc. on the site show that it was a very prosperous town till the end of 3rd century A. D., when it was probably abandoned. The kings in these documents have the title *devaputra,* which was used in India by the Kushans. The name of the city occurs in the documents as *Niña.* References are also made to Khotan in these documents under various names Khotamna, Khodana, Kustanaka. The names of persons occurring in them are purely Indian : Bhima Bangusena, Nandasena, Samusena, Sitaka, Upajiva etc. There are also local adaptations of Indian names : Angaca, Cuvatyalina, Phummaseva, Piteya, Sili, Sanghila, Samjaka etc. There are also some un-Indian names : Lipeya, Opgeya, Limira, etc.

With the help of the Chinese documents, archaeological evidences, and the information available from the ancient documents of Niya, it is now possible to make some general observations on the cultural life of the people of ancient Khotan. They were, we have seen, using the Indian script—since the early period up to the 3rd century A. D. it was definitely Kharosthi and later on Kharosthi was ousted by Brahmi, probably with the introduction of Sarvastivada Buddhism from Kashmir. As the archaeological evidences show, Buddhism was not unknown in Khotan, but it probably belonged to another school. The manuscript of Dharmapada in Kharosthi is written in a Prakrit, and certainly belonged to the school which had Prakrit as its sacred language. It might have been the Mahasanghika school, which had a number of convents in Khotan, as the Tibetan records say. Sarvastivada Buddhism and also Mahayana were introduced in all likelihood in the 4th century, as towards the end of that century Kumarajiva found it convenient to study the Tripitaka of that school and its Vibhasa in Kashgar which was on the gateway to Khotan.

The local language of Khotan was Eastern Iranian. Some would call it Śaka. Documents in this language have been discovered from the site of Dandan Uiliq, but all the documents belong to a late period, about the 8th century. About the language current in Khotan, the Tibetan Annals contain a very significant statement: "The common language agrees with neither India nor China. The letters agree successively with India. The manners of the laity agree for the most part with China. The clerical manners and the clerical language agree for the most part with India". The monks therefore cultivated the language of the Buddhist canon, in the early period Prakrit, and in the later Sanskrit. The kings and officials, as we can see from the Sino-Kharosthi coins and the Niya documents, used a sort of Prakrit closely allied to the Prakrit of North-Western India of the Kushan period. This shows that in the early period, the population of the kingdom of Khotan and the adjoining states contained a predominating Indian element. The Tibetan tradition also confirms it by mentioning that the kingdom was originally founded by colonisers from India and China.

Khotan rose to be an active centre of Buddhist studies very early. Already in the year 259 A. D. a Chinese monk named Chu She-hing came to Khotan for the study of Buddhism. Chu She-hing is a fairly well-known figure in the early history of Chinese Buddhism. It was he who compiled one of the first catalogues of Buddhist texts translated into Chinese. On account of difficulties in the interpretation of Buddhist texts that had already been translated into Chinese, he wanted to study Buddhism first-hand under good teachers. He was told that such teachers were to be found in Khotan. He came to Khotan and applied himself seriously to Buddhist studies. In a few years he collected 90 bundles of original Buddhist texts containing about 6000 words which he wanted to send to China. The local Buddhist scholars requested the king not to permit him to take the manuscripts to China, as they were afraid that the texts would be wrongly interpreted and misused. She-hing, however, got the permission to send the texts after proving that he understood the texts. She-hing, however, did not leave Khotan. He sent the texts with his disciple, Fu-ju-tan (Punyadhana ?), to China. She-hing died in Khotan at a ripe old age of 80 years.

The texts sent home by Chu She-hing were partly translated by a Khotanese Buddhist scholar, Mokṣala, who went to China in 291. He was assisted by an Indian monk, whose correct name probably was Śukla-ratna. The texts translated were *Pañcaviṁśati-sāhasrikā-Prajñāpāramitā*, *Vimalakīrtinirdeśa* and *Suraṅgama-sūtra*, all canonical texts of Mahayana. As the texts had been sent from Khotan by She-hing, it is clear that Khotan had become a seat of Mahayana studies already in the 3rd century.

In the beginning of the 5th century, a Buddhist scholar of Magadha, Dharmaksema, who was a profound student of Mahayana, was working in Leang-chou. He had brought from India an incomplete manuscript of the *Mahāparinirvāṇa-sūtra*. While translating the text into Chinese, he was told that the rest of the manuscript could be found in Khotan. He went to Khotan probably in 412 or 413, and found there the second part of the text which he brought to China. The text in 33 Chapters was translated between 414 and 421. After he had completed the translation, he was further told that the whole text contained 10000 verses, but he had translated only 35000. The entire text could be found only in Khotan, but he had no chance of returning to Khotan in search of the text.

About the same time a pupil of Dharmaksema, Tsiu-kiu King-sheng, who was a nobleman of Leang-chou, on hearing from Dharmaksema that Khotan was a great centre of Mahayana studies, went to Khotan. He settled down there in the Gomati-mahavihara and studied the Mahayana Buddhism with an Indian teacher named Buddhasena, who was a great teacher of Mahayana and "in all the countries of the West, was known as She-tseu (Simha) for all his attainments". On his return to China, King-sheng translated the texts which he had studied in Khotan and brought back with him. These were Mahayana texts on Dhyāna.

Soon after the return of King-sheng, eight Chinese monks of Leang-chou came to Khotan in 439 in search of Buddhist texts. They came to Khotan at a time when the Pancavārṣika assembly was being held, attended the lectures of some of the teachers there, and wrote down some texts from their dictation which they took back to China.

We know definitely that a number of important Buddhist texts had been taken to China from Khotan. Thus a monk named Fa-ling took to China from Khotan a manuscript of the famous *Avataṁsaka-sutra*, which was translated by Buddhabhadra in 418. A monk named Fa-hien brought from Khotan in 475 the manuscript of the *Saddharma-puṇḍarika*, which was also translated by Dharmamati in 490.

Khotan continued to play the same great role in the transmission of Buddhism to China even in the T'ang period. Siksananda was the greatest among the Buddhist scholars of Khotan to have gone to China. He reached China in 695 and worked there till his death in 710. He translated 19 texts in all, the most voluminous being the *Mahavaipulya* or the *Avatamsaka-sutra* in 80 chapters.

We know from various Chinese sources that the Khotanese were very fond of music and drama, and this also found expression in the annual Buddhist festival, Buddha-yatra, which was known in India and is still perpetuated in some form in Car festivals. Fa-hien gives a very vivid picture of this festival of Khotan. The monks of the Gomativihara were the leaders in the procession. Fa-hien yays :

"At a distance of 3 or 4 li from the city, a four-wheeled image-car is made, over thirty feet in height, looking like a movable Hall of Buddha, and adorned with the seven preciosities with streaming pennants and embroidered canopies. The image of Buddha is placed in the middle of the car with two attendant Bodhisattvas, while *devas* are made to follow in waiting, all brilliantly carved in gold and silver. When the images are one hundred paces from the city gate, the king takes off his Cap of State and puts on new clothes, walking bare-foot and holding flowers and incense in his hands with the attendants on each side, he proceeds out of the gate. On meeting the images, he bows his head down to the ground, scatters flowers and burns incense. When the images enter the city, the queen and court ladies who are on the top of the gate scatter far and wide all kinds of flowers which flutter down, and thus the splendour of decoration is complete. The cars are all different, each monastery has a day for its procession beginning on the first of the fourth month and lasting until the fourteenth. When processions end, the king and the queen go back to the palace".

FROM NIYA EASTWARDS

Hiuan-tsang, in his description of the country to the east of Niya, says that it was all desert. About 400 li to the east it was the old Tu-ho-lo country with its ruined cities which had long been deserted. About 600 li further to the East, the pilgrim visited Che-mo t'o-na, old country "with Nie-mo land" with lofty city walls but without an inhabitant. About 1000 li to the North-East was the old country of Na-fo-p'o, which was also known as Lou-lan.

The old Tu-ho-lo country as described by Hiuan-tsang was evidently an important territory in early times, which was situated in the deltaic region of the Tarim river and on the Southern route to Tunhuang. Due to natural causes like the expansion of the desert, erosion of arable lands and drying up of the rivers, the area became gradually deserted and the ancient cities fell in ruins. Explorations of Sir Aurel Stein read along with the information available from ancient Chinese history have led to the identification of the ancient sites.

The modern site called Endere represents the ancient Tu-ho-lo country mentioned by the pilgrim. The name stands for ancient Tukhara, Tochari of the Greek writers. But the appearance of the name in this area seems to be enigmatic. It may be supposed that they represented a branch of the Yue-ches who were settled in the region of Tunhuang, but they had been driven away from that area by the Huns in the 2nd century B. C., and had followed the Northern route in their retreat to the Oxus region. The

Endere site, as shown by the archaeological finds, was inhabited till the 3rd or 4th century. It is not, however, improbable that one of the branches of the Yue-che people (called Little Yue-che) had remained for some centuries in this area. It is also possible that the Indo-European Tukhara (Yue-che) people, in the course of their migration from the west to the Chinese frontier in the remote past, had first colonised this area. The Chinese accounts mention Yue-che families living in Tun-huang area as late as the 3rd. century A. D., and the Chinese documents, discovered from Lobnor region and belonging to the 4th century, still speak of Yue-che soldiers in Chinese pay and posted in the area. So the existence of Tukhara (Yue-che) in this region in the 4th century is well borne out by the archaeological finds. It is not, however, clear what Hiuan-tsang exactly meant by the "ancient Tu-ho-co (Tukhara) country." The archaeological finds from Endere have brought to light Kharosthi tablets and manuscripts of the type found in Niya. Ruins of a Buddhist stupa also show that Buddhism had been established in this area before its final abandonment.

The country further to the east, Che-mo-t'o-na and Tsiu-umo land mentioned by Hiuan-tsang is definitely identified from archaeological finds. Tsiu-mo is written as Tso-mo by Song-yun and as Nie-mo by Hiuan-tsang. Nie-mo, however, is only a copyist's mistake for Tsiu-mo. Tsiu-mo or Tso-mo is only a shortened form of the name Che-mo-t'o-na. The original name of the country was Calmadana, which is found in the Kharosthi documents from Niya. In fact the relation between Niya and Calmadana was very intimate. A Chinese document from Niya mentions a royal consort from Tsiu-mo or Calmadana. Modern Cherchen represents the old site of Calmadana. It is about 4 days' journey from Niya over a dreary part of the desert. The country is mentioned in the former Han Annals as lying on the high road from Shan-Shan or Lobnor region to the west. In Song-yun's time (beginning of the 6th century) the city was a city of 100 families. In this town there were, it is said, representations of a Buddha and Bodhisattva in pure Chinese style, which had been brought by Lukuang, who carried an expedition in the Tarim basin towards the end of the 4th century. Hiuan-tsang, as we have seen, found the place deserted, but it was soon after re-occupied by the Chinese army under the T'ang. The name of the town was changed from Tsiu-mo to Po-hsien about this time (674-676). Recent explorations have brought to light the ruins of a Buddhist stupa which show that the small town of Calmadana professed Buddhism in early times.

The more important towns lay to the north-east of Cherchen. Hiuan-tsang mentions this area as Na-fo-p'o which, according to him, was called in ancient times Lou-lan. This brings us to the region of Lobnor. Lobnor was situated on the oldest route connecting China with Central Asia. It stood on the shortest line of communication between Tunhuang and the Western countries (Niya, Khotan, etc) along the foot of the Kuruknag and the Lop desert. It is a fertile oasis in the delta of the Tarim river.

In the Han Annals, the name of the country is given as Shan-Shan, but it is said that the ancient name was Loulan. There were two chief cities in Shan-Shan, the one is called Yu-ni, "the old town," and the other Yi-Hsiun, "the new town". The Tibetan documents found in this area give the names of "Great Nob" and "Little Nob" to these towns respectively. Archaeological finds have led to the identification of the "Old town" with Charklik and the "new town" with Miran. The Chinese name Na-fu-p'o given by Hiuan-tsang seems to be the same as Nob of the Tibetan documents and Lop of modern times. Shan-Shan is a pure Chinese name to replace the old local name Loulan. Loulan was evidently a Chinese transcription of the original name Kroraina or Krorayina found in the Kharosthi documents. Kroraina in the Prakrit spoken in this area would give a dialectal form ke Lolaina, which was transcribed into Chinese.

The Chinese Annals give a fairly detailed account of ancient Kroraina. Under the former Hans, the country was known as Loulan, but the name was changed by the Chinese into Shan-Shan from 77 B. C. The neighbouring territories such as Tsu-mo

(Cherchen), Hsiao-yuan (on the road to Kucha in the north), Ching-chueh (Niya) were all dependencies of the state of Shan-Shan. In 119, Pan-yong planned to establish a military colony at Lou-lan. By establishing it, he wanted to dominate the West, control the roads to Karasahr and Kucha in the north, and in the south to fortify Shan-Shan and Khotan. The plan was to enable the kingdom of Shanshan to fight the Hiung-nus and safeguard the direct route from Tun-huang to the Western countries. Military colony was actually established in 124 A. D. Pan-yong came to Shan-Shan to receive there the submission of the kings of the various Western countries. Although the Chinese had changed the name of the country into Shan-Shan, the easternmost part of the country continued to be known under the old name Loulan (Kroraina).

Kroraina was a stronghold of Buddhism and Indian culture. Fa-hien tells us that there were 4000 monks, all followers of Hinayana in the country in his time. The common people, although Buddhists, were not so strict in the observance of the rules of India as the monks.

Kharosthi documents discovered from various sites of Kroraina are written in the Prakrit which was also current in Niya. It was the official language of the country. These records contain personal names of Indian derivation as well as of local origin. Names of Indian derivation are : Anamdasena, Bhatisana, Bhimaya, Budhamitra, Dhamñapala, Kumudvati, Pumñadeva, Caraka, Rutra, Sujada, Vasudeva. Names of local origin such as : Cauleya, Cuvalayina, Kapgeya, Kalpisa, Kipsa etc. The documents contain also loan words from Iranian and a few Central Asian languages.

The Buddhist shrines of Miran are of great importance. Whereas the sculpture is mainly of the Gandhara style, the mural paintings reveal also Western influence. We get representations of winged angels as in early Christian art. One of the mural paintings is attributed to one Tita (titasa na ghali hastakrica), who seems to have been Titus. The painting reveals definite Hellenistic influence. The silk banners discovered from Miran contain Kharosthi inscriptions, which show that they were given to the Buddhist shrine in token of pious wish for the recovery of persons.

Most of the names are Indian—Asagosa, Caraka, Caroka(Caruka), Samanay (Sramanaka). There are also some Iranian names : Friyana, Firina, and Mitraka.

The Chinese documents prove that Kroraiana was occupied till the 4th century ; the last dated Chinese document is of 312-313. The frescoes, banners and other antiquities bearing Kharosthi inscriptions also belong to that period. We get from the Kharosthi documents the names of at least five kings of a dynasty which reigned in Kroraina in the 3rd century A. D. These are : Pepiya, Tajaka, Aṁgoka, Mahiri and Vaṣmana. Aṁgoka and Mahiri had long reigns. They use the royal titles of the Kushans such as : Maharaya, Raytiraya, Devaputra, Dharmia, Mahaṁta etc.

CHAPTER IV

EASTERN TURKESTAN — THE NORTHERN STATES

BHARUKA AND KUCI

In ancient times there were four states in the northern part of the Tarim basin which were culturally united. These states from west to east are mentioned under the following names in the records of Hiuan-tsang : Po-lu-kia, K'iu-che, A-ki-ni and Kao-ch'ang. About Po-lu-kia, the pilgrim says that the character of its people, their customs, literature were the same as those of K'iu-che. The languages of the two countries were also almost the same. About K'iu-che and A-ki-ni, he says that the writing of both the countries was similar to that of India with some differences. About Kao-ch'ang he does not say much, as it was in his times largely under Chinese influence, but there is no doubt that in earlier times it belonged to the same cultural zone as that of the three other states.

Po-lu-kia, in earlier Chinese texts, is mentioned under the names Ki-me and K'u-me, which were, in all probability, based on the Turkish word Kum, which means "Sand," "desert". In the Han Annals, the place is described as the source of such minerals as copper, iron and orpiment. The original name of Po-lu-kia is found in some Sanskrit documents of Central Asia as Bharuka. It has been identified with modern Aksu. It was probably a wrong Sanskritisation ; the original name seems to have been Baluka, which had the same meaning as Turkish Kum "Sand." The northern route here bifurcated, one going towards Kashgar, and the other through the Bedal Pass towards Western Turkestan.

The name of K'iu-che is also found under three other forms — Kiu-tse, Kuei-tse and Kiu-yi. This is modern Kucha. The Sanskrit form of the name is found as Kucī in some of the Sanskrit documents discovered from Central Asia. The kings of Kuci are mentioned in the same documents as Kucimaharaja.

The kingdom of A-ki-ni is mentioned in earlier Chinese sources under the names : Yen-k'i, Wu-k'i and Wu-yi. All these names are connected with Sanskrit Agni or its derivatives. In fact, the Sanskrit form of the name is found in the Sanskrit documents above referred to as Agni. Its kings are mentioned as Agni-maharaja. The country has been identified with modern Karasahr.

Further east, Kao-ch'ang, in Han times, was called Kiu-she. It was divided by the T'ien-shan into two Zones, one was Kiu-she, anterior or inner and the other Kiu-she, posterior or outer. The name of the country was changed into Kao-ch'ang from the beginning of the 4th century. The anterior part of Kiu-she is identified with modern Turfan, whereas the other part with Guchen. Turfan was certainly the more important of the two.

Uigur texts speak of Kucha and its adjoining countries as four *Küsan.* One of the texts is said to have been translated from the *idivut* (*itivuttaka*) of Vaibhasika Acarya, *Klianzini* (*Kalyāna-sena*) which was in Küsan original. The other texts speak of the following Buddhist teachers of fame of the country of four Küsan : *Budarakisiti* (*Buddharakṣita*), *Sarvarakisiti* (*Sarvarakṣita*) and *Azokrakisiti* (*Asokarakṣita*). This Turkish name of Kucha is also found in a Sanskrit-Chinese Dictionary of the T'ang period under the name *Kucīnaṁ* or *Kucīna*, being the genitive plural form of the name. The ancient name of Turfan, Kiu-she, also seems to have been of the same origin. The archaic pronunciation of the name would give a form like Kiwo-ṣi (Kuṣi, Kuci) from which a genitive plural form of the name would be Küsana.

These evidences would show that the people of the four states of Aksu, Kucha, Karasahr and Turfan were of the same stock in ancient times, spoke the same language with probably some dialectal differences and shared the same cultural life. Their language may be termed as Kuchean or, according to the Turkish nomenclature, Küsana. The specimens of this language have been discovered from various sites in Kucha and Karasahr. That this language was spoken in Karasahr is also proved by the fact that a number of mural inscriptions in old sites of Karasahr is in this language.

This Kuchean or Küsana language, we have seen, is akin to the Tokharian or the language of ancient Tokharestan. The specimens of ancient Tokharian have also been discovered in the neighbourhood of Karasahr and also in Turfan where, according to all appearance, they had been carried either by the

Turks or the Buddhist priests of Tokharestan in the 9th century after the Arab conquest of Tokharestan. The Turks had set up a new empire with Turfan as the centre in the 9th century after their downfall in Tokharestan, and here they tried to preserve their ancient Buddhist heritage. Hence the Tokharian texts are found along with Uigur translations. It is almost certain that the local language of this region in earlier times was Kuchean.

The two languages we have said are dialects of a hitherto unknown branch of the Indo-European. Kuchean, however, preserves its more archaic form as it was not so much contaminated by other languages. But Tokharian in Tokharestan underwent greater phonetic decay under the influence of Iranian languages. Thus, in Kuchean, we have for Buddha : *Püdnakte*, but in Tokharian *Ptankte*, Kuchean— *kwipe*, Tokharian — *kip*, Kuchean —*Kliyaus*, Tokharian—*Klyos* etc. The common origin of the two languages is further pointed out by their similar names : the language of Kucha, the Kuchean (Tokharian B of the German scholars) was, we have seen, Küsan, and that of Tokharestan, Toxri (Tokharian A) was the language of the Kushans ; Kuṣana.

CONFLICTS WITH CHINA

Of the history of the four northern states, we know a good deal from the Chinese sources. These sources speak in greater detail about Kucha which was the most powerful of the four states and played the same great rôle in the North as Khotan in the South in the dissemination of Indian culture to the Tarim basin and to China. The three other states play a secondary rôle in this history.

We will now try to reconstruct the history of Kucha with the available materials from the Chinese sources. The Annals of the former Han dynasty contain the following information on Kucha : "The king of Kucha has his capital in the city called Yen. The kingdom has a population of nearly 81,317. The number of good soldiers is 21,076. There are various officials of high status beginning with a Commander-in-Chief down to interpreters. In the South, the country borders on Tsing-tsiue, in the South-East

Tsiu-mo, in the South-West Yu-mi, in the north Wu-sun, and in the West Ku-mo. The people are clever in smelting of different metals."

"Formerly General Li Kuang-li went on a punitive expedition against Ta-yuan (102 B. C.). On his way back he passed by Yu-mi (Keriya) ; Yu-mi was to send their heir-apparent Lai-tan as a hostage to Kucha. Li Kuang-li blamed Kucha by saying : 'All the foreign countries are subjects of the Han. Why should Kucha receive a hostage from Yu-mi ?' Thereafter, taking Lai-tan with him, he returned to the capital. Emperor Chao-ti (86-74 B. C.) appointed the heir-apparent Lai-tan as Deputy Governor-General, and he ordered him to colonise Lun-Ta'i (Bugur, a place between Kucha and Karasahr). A nobleman of Kucha, Ku-yin, thus addressed the king of Kucha — 'Lai-tan formerly was a subject of our kingdom. Now he has received official appointment from the Hans and has come to put us to trouble by colonising. This will bring evil upon us.' Thereupon Lai-tan was killed by the king and a letter of apology was sent to the Chinese Emperor. The Chinese could not punish Kucha. During the reign of Siuan-ti, (73-49 B. C.) the Chinese army was sent to the country of the Wu-sun. The Chinese General, on his return journey, raised an army of 50,000 and prepared to attack Kucha on the ground that the king of Kucha had killed Lai-tan, who was the Deputy Governor. The king of Kucha apologised by saying that that had occurred during the time of his predecessor on the erroneous advice of Ku-yin, but that he was innocent. Ku-yin was thereupon taken to the Chinese General and put to death.

Friendly relation between Kucha and China soon became strengthened. A Wu-sun princess, who was connected with the Chinese imperial family on the mother's side, was married to Kiang-pin, the king of Kucha. In 65 B. C., Kiang-pin went to the Chinese court to pay his homage. Relation between the Chinese court and Kucha henceforth became more frequent, After the death of Kiang-pin, his son Ch'eng-to called himself a grandson of the Han. During the reign of Ch'eng-ti (32-1 B. C.) the Chinese emperor continued to consider the kings of Kucha as near relatives.

Kucha, in this period, benefited by the opening of a trade route through the country. The northern route from Yu-men to Kashgar passed by Kucha. In 2 B. C., another route, which passed by Turfan and followed the foothills of the T'ien-shan, was made to converge on Kucha before proceeding to the west. This immensely contributed to the prosperity of Kucha.

After the fall of the Former Hans in 24 A. D., the small states of the Tarim basin submitted to the Hiung-nu (Huns). It was then that Hien, the king of So-k'iu (Cokkuka, Karghalik), who was a great ally of China, invaded Kucha. This invasion took place in 41 A. D. He attacked Kucha on several occasions. Other states also were frightened. In 46 A. D., Hien directed another attack against Kucha, killed the king and annexed the kingdom. He placed his son Tso-lo on the throne of Kucha. The western portion was separated and another state founded with Wu-lei (Bugur) as capital. Hien appointed Sse-kien (who was also called king of Kuei-sai) as its king. After a few years a revolution broke out and both Tso-lo and Sse-kien were killed. The Hiung-nu appointed Shen-tu (Induk), a nobleman (probably of Indian origin, as the name indicates) of Kucha as king of the country. Since then Kucha became a dependency of the Hiung-nu.

In 73 A. D., Kien was made king of Kucha by the Hiung-nu. With the help of the barbarian races he assured the safety of the Northern route, attacked Su-le (Kashgar), conquered it, killed its king and appointed Tou-t'i, a man of Kucha as king of Su-le. The very next year (74 A. D.) a Chinese army under Pan-Ch'ao appeared on the scene, and Tou-t'i was surprised and taken prisoner. Pan-Ch'ao assembled all the generals and officers of Kashgar, told them about the unjust attitude of Kucha, and set up Chong, the son of the elder brother of the last king as king of Kashgar. Since then the enmity between Kashgar and Kucha became accentuated.

Emperor Ming of the Han dynasty died in 75 A.D. Taking advantage of this, the king of Yen-ki (Karasahr) attacked and killed the Chinese Governor-General. About the same time, Kucha and Aksu also attacked Kashgar. Pan-Ch'ao was again advised to return to quell the rebellion of the Tarim states. Pan-Ch'ao first came to Khotan where he was welcomed by the people as their defender. He next marched on to Kashgar, as after his departure the two cities of Kashgar had submitted to Kucha. In 78 A. D., Pan-Ch'ao at the head of a combined army of Kashgar, Sogdiana, Khotan and other states first attacked Aksu and She-ch'ang (Uch-Turfan) and defeated them. As all the states excepting Kucha and Karasahr had submitted to him he sent a request to the emperor to send him reinforcement to enable him to attack those two countries. If those countries could be defeated, he pointed out, then the route to the Pamirs would be freed. He further suggested to appoint Po Pa, the son of the king of Kucha who was a hostage at the Chinese court, as the king of Kucha and send him to his help at the head of a native army. He had good support from the people of Aksu and Wen-su (Uch-Turfan) as Kucha had nominated two foreigners as kings of those two countries.

Pan-Ch'ao's plan was approved. Preparations were also made by Kucha to meet the Chinese army, but the Kuchean army was defeated in a decisive battle near Kashgar, in 88 A. D. Kucha made another effort to get the help of the Great Yue-ches of Tokharestan in order to strengthen her forces. In 90 A. D., the Yue-ches, in fact, sent a large army by the Pamir route. This army went short of provision in course of the difficult crossing when Pan-Ch'ao fell upon them and completely routed them. Next year Kucha, Aksu and Uch-Turfan, all submitted to Pan-Ch'ao. The king of Kucha, Yu-li-t'o was deposed and Po Pa was set up as king. A Chinese Governor-General was placed at Kucha to look after the local affairs. Unrest started in various states again in 106, and the people of Kucha also revolted against the Governor-General and his protegee king, Po Pa. Kucha was besieged by the army of Kucha, Aksu and Uch-Turfan. Ultimately the rebels were defeated, Kucha was pacified.

In 124, when another Chinese expedition was sent to the Tarim basin, the king of Kucha, Po Ying, with kings of Aksu and Uch-Turfan, gave his friendly help to the Chinese, and this led to the ultimate defeat of the Hiung-nus, who were still occupying the territories to the north of the T'ien-shan. Henceforth, for nearly a century Kucha is not heard of in Chinese history. Kucha was evidently entertaining friendly relations with China. In 224, we hear of Kucha again sending an ambassador with presents to the Chinese court. In this period, Aksu and Uch-Turfan were dependencies of Kucha.

Under the Tsin (265-316), Kucha continued to entertain friendly relations with China. In 285, the king of Kucha sent his son to the Chinese court to enter the imperial service. During the first quarter of the 4th century Kucha also sent embassies to China. It was about this time that enmity broke out between Kucha and Karasahr, and Long Huei, the king of Karasahr, attacked Kucha, killed, king Po Shan and subjugated his territories. For some years Long Huei was the master of the Tarim basin. He, however, was subsequently murdered by a Kuchean named Lo-yun.

In the period 350-394, China sent a military expedition under General Lu-Kuang. The expedition was directed against Kucha for her allegiance to the old rulers. Kucha was invaded in 382. King Po Shun refused to submit, and the gates of the city were closed. All the inhabitants of the city were under arms. The barbarians, (probably the Hiung-nu) and also the army of Uch-Turfan came to his help. But Lu-Kuang won a decisive battle against all of them, and King Po Shun fled with his treasures. Lu-Kuang then entered the city, all the chiefs made their submission to him and Po Chen, the son of the younger brother of Po Shun, was installed as king. Lu-Kuang returned to Leang-chou with a large number of prisoners amongst whom was found the famous Buddhist scholar Kumarajiva, who was destined to play a very significant role in the history of Chinese Buddhism.

During the Wei period (386-534), the relations between China and Kucha again became strained. Kucha, at the beginning in 437 and 439, sent embassies to China with presents, but soon the Chinese emperor found it necessary to send an expedition against that country. The expedition was sent in 448. Kucha also sent an army under Wu-kie-mu-ti to offer battle. The Kuchean army was, however, defeated. Kucha renewed the practice of sending embassies with presents to the Chinese court. Thus Kuchean embassies were sent in 449, 475, 477, 479, 510, 518 and 522. Abut the same time Kucha also sent embassies to the rulers of South China in 511, and 521. The reigning king of Kucha in 521 was called Ni-jue-mo-chu-na-sheng.

After the fall of the Wei, the Chou dynasty ruled in North China from 577 to 581. Embassy was sent from Kucha also in this period. With the rise of the T'ang dynasty Kucha continued to entertain the same friendly relation as before. King Su-fa Pu-kiu sent an ambassador to Emperor Kaó-tsu in the period 618-627. The next king of Kucha was the son of the former king and was named Su-fa Tie. He had a surname : She-kien mo-ho-se-li-fa. Su-fa Tie sent an embassy in 630. It was about this time that Hiuan-tsang passed through Kucha. Hiuan-tsang says that the kings of Kucha were of the Kiu-che (Kuchean) race and mentions two kings of the country. About one of them he says "In recent times there was a king called Gold-Flower who exhibited rare penetration into the Buddhist doctrines". The other was King A-chu-ni-, who possessed supernatural power.

After the death of Su-fa Tie, who sent an embassy to China in 630, his younger brother Ho-li Pu-she-pi ascended the throne. He sent embassies twice in the year 647. But soon an expedition was sent against Kucha, because Kucha had helped in the revolt of Karasahr against the Chinese authority. The Turkish chief who had accepted the vassalage of the Chinese emperor was entrusted with this expedition. The Kuchean army led by Kie-lie-tien was totally defeated and the city was besieged. During this campaign, all the cities of Kucha were destroyed and a large number of inhabitants were put to the sword. The Turkish chief put She-hu, the younger brother of the king on the throne. King Ho-li Pu-she-pi, his general Kie-lie-tien and the minister Na-li were sent to China as captives. A few years later the Emperor, Kao-tsong, released them, restored the kingdom to Ho-li-pu-she-pi, who was allowed to go back with his two attendants. The king came to China once again to pay homage to the emperor, but he could not go back to Kucha on account of a court intrigue by Na-li and Kie-lie-tien. On the death of Ho-li-pu-she-pi, his son Su-ki was appointed king by an imperial mandate. Su-ki sent an embassy in 674.

In 692, the king of Kucha, Yen-tien-tie came personally to pay homage to the emperor. It was at this time that the Tibetans drove away the Chinese from the southern part of the Tarim basin, and extended their conquests as far as Karasahr. The Chinese headquarters were removed to Kucha from Turfan. We hear of embassies still going from Kucha in 709, and in 719 when the king, Po Mo-pi, died, and was succeeded by his son To-tsa in 730 when the brother of the king came to the court in 747 and 748. When Wu-k'ong passed through Kucha in 787 or 788, the king of Kucha was Po Hoan.

Kucha is again mentioned in the Chinese records for a brief period towards the beginning of the 11th century. Embassies were sent from Kucha in 1001, 1010, 1013, 1017, 1024, 1031, 1029, 1037, 1071, 1096. But the rulers in this period were of the Uigur stock, the title of their kings was "Lion-King." The old rulers had passed away long ago.

AGNIDESA OR KARASAHR

We have seen that the kingdom of Karasahr politically was intimately connected with Kucha, and very often the two states were allies in resisting the Chinese aggression and maintaining their independence. The Chinese accounts therefore contain some references to the political condition of Karasahr from the Han times to the end of the T'ang. During the first expansion of the Chinese supremacy under Emperor Wu-ti (140-87 B. C.) Karasahr first sent an ambassador to China and recognized the Chinese suzerainty. But Karasahr threw off the Chinese yoke towards the end of the 1st century before Christ. But soon after, as both Kucha and So-k'iu (Cokkuka-Karghalik) submitted to China, Karasahr had also to follow suit. In the 1st cent. A. D. trouble again broke out, and in 75 A. D. the king of Karasahr, Shuen, and his son Chong revolted against Chinese authority, killed the Chinese Governor and his retinue. But the expedition of Pan-Ch'ao again reduced these states to the Chinese vassalage. Kuang, the king of Karasahr, was killed, the city was sacked and the people were treated with great cruelty. An officer of Karasahr, Yuang Mong, who was a hostage in Chinese court, was placed on the throne of Karasahr in 94 A. D. He, on his return, revolted against the Chinese authority between 121 and 125, but was defeated by the Chinese expeditionary force in 127 and sent his own son to the Chinese court with presents. Since then Karasahr entertained friendly relations with China for some time.

An embassy was sent to the Chinese court in 220. In 285, King Long An sent his son to the court to be enrolled in the Imperial guard. Another son of Long An, Huei, waged war against the various states of the Tarim basin and was master of Kucha for some years. His son Hi was defeated by the Chinese in 345. About 386, the king of Karasahr, Ni-liu, paid homage to Ku Kuang, who had declared himself emperor at Leang-chou. Embassies came to China from Karasahr in 437, 439 and 448, but China, dissatisfied with the vascillating policy of Karasahr, sent an expeditionary force, and its king, Kiu-she-pei-na, fled to Kucha.

For nearly a century nothing is heard about Karasahr in the Chinese Annals. We hear of embassies coming from Karasahr only in 564 and 606. The king who was ruling in 606 was Long Tu-k'i. Hiuan-tsang, who visited Karasahr in 629, speaks in details about the culture and the religion, but practically nothing about its political condition.

The Annals of the T'ang dynasty on several occasions mention Karasahr. In 632, King Long Tu-k'i-che sent an embassy to the court. On the request of the king, the shorter route to China through the desert was opened by the Chinese authorities. The intention was to isolate Turfan, through which the route passed formerly. Turfan was slowly passing under the influence of the Uigurs and interfering in the normal relations between China and the Tarim states. The king of Turfan was defeated by the Chinese army in 640, and compelled to release those inhabitants of Karasahr who were held as prisoners.

But soon after, Karasahr also passed under Uigur influence and contracted a treaty of alliance with them. Karasahr cut off relations with China. But the younger brothers of the king Hie-pi,

She-hu and Li-p'o-chun intrigued with the Chinese and joined the Chinese expeditionary force against Karasahr. Karasahr was defeated, and king Tu-k'i-che was brought as prisoner to China. Li-p'o-chun was appointed king of Karasahr. But the Uigurs invaded Karasahr again and deposed Li-p'o-chun. The throne was restored to the latter soon after by the people of Karasahr. A relative of the king, Sie-p'o A-na-che entered into conspiracy with the king of Kucha, usurped the throne and handed over Li-p'o-chun as prisoner to the king of Kucha, who put him to death. Another Chinese expedition was sent against Karasahr. A brother of Tu-k'i-che, P'o-k'ie-li was set up as king in 648. On the latter's death, Tu-k'i-che, who was a hostage in China, was sent back to Karasahr to ascend the throne. On his death, Long Lai-tu became the king and ruled till 719. His successor was Yen-t'u-fu-yen. Karasahr is heard of as sending embassies to China till the period 742-755, after which it was conquered by the Tibetans and all connections between Karasahr and China ceased.

KAO-CH'ANG OR TURFAN

We have seen that Turfan and its counterpart, Guchen to the north of the T'ien-shan, formed, till the beginning of the 4th century, one political unit. Throughout the Han period, both the territories under the name Kiu-she were considered to be the gateway to the West. In the time of Emperor Wu-ti (160-108 B. C.), the southern part of the territory, which is Turfan, submitted to China and accepted a Chinese administration. But the northern part, Guchen, continued to remain defiant under the domination of the Hiung-nus, the eternal enemies of the Chinese. The Hiung-nus were completely defeated by the Chinese in 89 A. D., and since then Guchen also came to owe its allegiance to China. War between the two parts of the territory was frequent, and it was with Chinese help that Turfan could maintain its existence. Thus in 96 A. D. when Wei-pei-ta, king of Turfan, was attacked by the army of Guchen, he had to ask for Chinese help. The Hiung-nus continued to create trouble in Guchen from time to time till the end of the Han period. In 280 A. D. the king of Turfan sent his son to the Chinese court.

From the beginning of the 4th century, the name of the southern part of the territory was changed into Kao-ch'ang by the Chinese, and that is actual Turfan. In 386. king of Turfan, Mi-ti, went himself to the Chinese capital with his Rājyaguru, Kumārabuddhi. to request the Emperor to send a Governor-General. In consequence of the expedition of Lu-Kuang against Kucha, an independent office of Chinese Governor was established in Kan-su. Turfan in this period was brought directly under the Chinese rule. It continued to remain so till 460 when the legitimate ruling line of Turfan got back the kingdom. We get the names of some of the local rulers of this period : K'an Po-chou (killed in 477), Yi-ch'eng, Shou-kuei (killed in 481), Chang Mong-ming, and Ma-Jou, etc. In 507, a Chinese dynasty under the name K'iu was established in Turfan, and the Chinese henceforth became masters of the country. The following kings of the K'iu dynasty are known from different sources :

K'iu-Kiu	497-520
„ Kuang	521-530
„ Kien	531-547
„ Hiuen li	548-554
„ Meon	555-560
„ Han ku	561-601
„ Po Ya	602-623
„ Wen t'ai	624-640
„ Che Mou	640

In 640, Turfan was brought under direct Chinese control. After a long war between the Tibetans, Chinese and Uigurs, the Uigurs became masters of Turfan in 870, and established their capital in Turfan at Qara Khodjo. Under the Uigurs, Turfan played a very important part in the history of Central Asia.

From the accounts discussed above, it is clear that Kucha played the most important role in the history of the northern part of Tarim basin for nearly one thousand years. Both Karasahr and

Turfan were the first lines of defence against Chinese agression which Kucha resisted whenever possible. In this task of preserving their culture and independence Kucheans had close allies in their consanguineous peoples of Aksu and Uch-Turfan in the west and of Karasahr in the east. Turfan, before it went under complete Chinese control, also was a feeble ally of Kucha.

From the dynastic names of the rulers of these territories we can easily find out that they belonged to a distinct race. The Chinese accounts clearly say that the ruling dynasty of Kucha was called "Po" which in Chinese means "White." If it was a Chinese translation of a local designation, it was probably used to distinguish the race as a white one. The names of Kuchean kings in the T'ang period had been Sanskritised. From the old Kuchean documents we get the name of King Swarnate (Suvarṇadatta ?), which seems to have been transcribed into Chinese as Su-fa-tie, who ruled in the first quarter of the 7th century. His father had the name of Su-fa-pu-kiue (Swarna or Suvarṇa—). His brother had the name of Ho-li-pu-she-pi (Haripuṣpa). Hiuan-tsang mentions a former ruler of Kucha under the name "Gold-Flower", which was certainly Suvarṇa-puṣpa. So far as the ruling dynasty of Karasahr is concerned, we have seen that it had the name of "Long", which is a Chinese word meaning Dragon (Sanskrit 'Naga). The names of private persons also had been Sanskritised in this area in the T'ang period. We get such names from the ancient documents as : Wiryamitre (Vīryamitra), Wiryasene (Vīryasena), Jñanasene, Mokṣacandre, etc.

BUDDHIST CULTURE

It is Buddhism which brought Sanskrit influence to the countries of the north. We do not know exactly when Buddhism was introduced in Kucha, but it could not have been much later than the end of the 1st century A. D. We get a full picture of Buddhism in Kucha from about the 3rd century, and that presupposes that Buddhism must have been introduced at least a century earlier to take root in the soil of Kucha. The annals of the Tsin dynasty (265-316) say that in this period there were nearly one thousand

Buddhist stupas and temples in Kucha. It was also in this period that Buddhist monks of Kucha started going to China. Po Yen, who was probably a member of the Kuchean royal family, became a Buddhist monk and came to the Chinese capital in 256-260. He translated six Buddhist texts into Chinese in 258 in the famous Buddhist temple of Po-ma-sse at Lo-yang. Po Śrimitra, who was also of Kuchean origin, went to China during the period 307-312, and then on account of political troubles moved to South China, where he translated three Buddhist texts between 335 and 342. We hear of another Kuchean prince of the name of Po-yen, who went to Leang-chou in 273. He was also a Buddhist scholar of repute, and knew a number of foreign languages. He has not, however, left any translation behind.

The fourth century was a period of great Buddhist activities in Kucha. In one of the Chinese texts relating to this period it is said that Kucha was almost entirely a Buddhist city. The palace of the king looked like a Buddhist monastery with standing images of Buddha carved in stone. Number of monasteries in the capital was very large, and there were also some special monasteries founded by the kings. There was a monastery called Ta-mu which had 170 monks. The monastery on the Po-shan hill in the north which was called Che-hu-li had 50 or 60 monks. The new monastery of the king of Wen-su (Uch-Turfan) had 70 monks. All these four monasteries were under the direction of Fu-t'u-she-mi (Buddhasvamin). The monks had to change their residence every three months. Unless they had passed at least five years after their ordination, they were not permitted to stay in the new monastery of the king even for one night. This new monastery of the king had 90 monks. The text also refers to a young monk of this monastery called Kiu-kiu (sic. mo)-lo (i. e. Kumāra) who was a great scholar and had studied the Mahayana. Buddhasvamin was his teacher, but while Buddhasvamin was a follower of the Āgamas (Hinayana), his disciple had become a follower of Mahayana.

The text further refers to other establishments of Kucha. There was the monastery of A-li (Āraṇyaka ?) with 180 nuns. There were also the monasteries of Liun-jo-kan with 50 and A-li-po with 30 nuns. These nunneries were also under the direction of Buddhasvamin as, according to the rule of the country, the nuns were not allowed to manage their own affairs. The nuns who inhabited these three monasteries were the daughters and the wives of the kings and nobles of 'the countries to the east of the Pamirs' (i. e. of the Tarim basin). "Out of piety they come to these monasteries to live a religious life. They observe very strict rules of discipline. They do not stay in the same residence for more than three months. They cannot go out unless led by three senior nuns. They have 500 rules for their observance".

The younger scholar of genius, Kumara, mentioned in the text, was no other than Kumarajiva. The biography of Kumarajiva preserved in Chinese sources also throws a good deal of light on the condition of Buddhism in Kucha. His father, Kumarayana, was an Indian, and his family was a family of ministers of this state. Kumarayana, however, abdicated his rights in favour of his relatives, embraced Buddhism and left for foreign countries. After crossing the difficult routes of the Pamirs he came to Kucha. He was warmly received by the king and was soon appointed Rajaguru. It was then that Jiva, a princess of the royal family, fell in love with Kumarayana. They were ultimately married, and one of the issues of this union was Kumarajiva. Soon after the birth of Kumarajiva, Jiva embraced Buddhism and became a nun. The monastery to which she retired was called Tsio-li, about 40 li to the north of Kucha. It was in this monastery that Jīva learnt the language of India.

When Jiva joined the Buddhist church with her son, Kumarajiva was only 7 years old. He started to learn by memory the sacred texts and could soon recite a number of Sutras and 1000 Gathas. Then he started learning Abhidharma. When he was nine years of age, his mother left with him for Kashmir with a view to give him better education. In Kashmir, Kumarajiva had the good luck to get a famous teacher, Bandhudatta, who was the cousin of the king of Kashmir. He taught the young disciple the Madhyama and Dirgha Āgamas. After three years of study, Kumarajiva's mother wanted to return with him to Kucha. Their route passed through the kingdom of the Yue-ches (Tokharestan). They then reached Sha-le (Kashgar).

Kumarajiva stayed in Kashgar for one year and studied the whole Abhidharmapiṭaka with the Kashmirian scholar, Buddhayaśas, who was then at Kashgar. He studied there also the four Vedas, five sciences, the Brahmanical Śastras and astronomy. It was at this time that two distinguished persons came there to study under him and to get their ordination. They were the two sons of King Tsan-kiun, the son of the king of So-kiu (Cokkuka). The two princes were called Suryasoma and Surya-bhadra. Suryasoma, who was the younger of the two, was a follower of Mahayana. Kumarajiva also studied the *Śataśāstra* and the *Madhyamaka-śāstra* etc. before leaving Kashgar.

On leaving Kashgar, they reached Wen-su (Uch-Turfan), which was the northern limit of Kucha. Here Kumarajiva defeated a Taoist teacher in controversy. The king of Kucha, Po Shun, came personally to Uch-Turfan to receive him, and take him back to Kucha. The daughter of the king, A-kie-ye-mo-ti, (Akṣayamati ?) , at that time became a nun and Kumarajiva explained to her the *Mahāsannipāta* and the *Mahāvaipulya-sūtras.*

On attaining the age of 20, Kumarajiva received full ordination in the king's palace. At this time there were 10,000 monks in Kucha. Kumarajiva lived in the New Monastery built by King Po Shun. By the side of this monastery in the old palace he discovered a manuscript of the *Pañcavimśati-Sāhasrikā Prajñā-pāramitā.* He explained the Mahayana Sutras in the great monastery of Tsio-li. A Kashmirian scholar, Vimalaksa, came to Kucha at this time and was received by Kumarajiva. The latter studied the Sarvastivada Vinayapiṭaka with Vimalaksa. Kumarajiva's mother now went back to India to pass the rest of her life with the permission of King Po Shun.

Kucha was invaded and destroyed by the Chinese expeditionary force under Lu-Kuang in 382, and a large number of prisoners were taken to Leang-chou by the victor. Kumarajiva was among these prisoners. At first he was much ill-treated by Lu Kuang. But soon when his merits were recognised, Lu Kuang treated him with respect and kept him at Leang-chou till 401. At the repeated request of the Emperor, he was then sent to Ch'ang-ngan, where he worked till his death in 413. He translated there

98 texts, and with him started a glorious epoch in the history of Chinese Buddhism.

Vimalaksa, who was staying in Kucha all this time, joined Kumarajiva in China in 404. A few years later, another Indian scholar named Dharmamitra came to Kucha, stayed there for a few years, and then went to Tun-huang. He reached the Chinese capital in 424. Among the personal friends of Kumarajiva, the Kashmirian scholar, Buddhayasa, under whom Kumarajiva had studied in Kashgar, joined him there. He was also joined in China by another Kashmirian scholar, Buddhabhadra. Kumarajiva was the centre of attraction, first in Kucha and then in the capital of China, for a number of years.

Kumarajiva was responsible for introducing Mahayana in the countries of the Tarim basin, and also in China in an authoritative manner. He was one of the greatest exponents of this form of Buddhism and also of the Madhyamika philosophy. He introduced all these texts in China through his beautiful translations. His services were evidently recognised by many Mahayana teachers of this period, who were responsible for interpolating the name of Kucha in some of the canonical Mahayana texts. Thus, in the Chinese translation of the *Candragarbhasūtra*, which is part of the Mahasannipata, in connection with the various manifestations of Buddha, we are told that Kucha had 99 manifestations whereas Aksu had 24. According to this text, Kucha had her divine protectors. Amongst the constellations, Śravaṇā was the protector of Kucha. So Kucha received a special place of honour in the Buddhist texts too, and that was an honour shown to the memory of Kumarajiva.

Towards the end of the 6th century, another Indian scholar, Dharmagupta, came to Kucha and stayed there in the king's monastery for two years. The king, who was a great believer in Mahayana, was much attached to him. Dharmagupta taught various Śastras in Kucha, including the *Tarkaśāstra*, before leaving for China. Hiuan-tsang passed through Kucha in 630. He tells us that in his times there were about 100 monasteries in Kucha with more than 5000 disciples. They were all followers of the Sarvastivada school of Hinayana. They were strict followers of the Buddhist customs of India, and read the original texts in Sanskrit. Among the specially famous monasteries, Hiuan-tsang mentions a few: About 40 li to the north of the city there were two monasteries on the slope of the mountain which were called Chao-hu-li (the same as Tsio-li of other accounts). The monastery contained a remarkably beautiful image of Buddha. The monks living there were pure, truthful and diligent in the discharge of ther duties.

Hiuan-tsang saw two standing images of Buddha outside the western gate of the city which were about 90 feet high. The quinquennial assemblies used to be held in the quadrangle in front of these images. Hiuan-tsang mentions another famous monastery called A-she-li-ni which stood nearby. This monastery was a great meeting-place of Buddhists from all countries. Hiuan-tsang says: "The hall of this temple is open and spacious. The image of Buddha is beautifully carved. The disciples are grave and decorous and very diligent in their duties. Rude and rough come together; the aged priests are learned and of great talent, and so from distant spots, the most eminent men who desire to acquire just principles come here and fix their abode. The king and his ministers and the great men of the realm offer to these priests the four sorts of provision, and their celebrities spread farther and farther."

The chief priest of the monastery of A-she-li-ni was Mo-ch'a-kiu-to (Mokṣagupta), who was the host of Hiuan-tsang. Hiuan-tsang tells us that Mokṣagupta had won the respect of all the different schools of religion by his rare ability and intelligence. He had travelled in India for twenty years, studied there, and specialised in the *Śabdavidyāśāstra*. From the information supplied to the pilgrim by him it appears that the Buddhist libraries of Kucha were very well equipped, and contained amongst others such books as: *Samyukta-hṛdaya, Abhidharmakośa* and *Vibhāṣā*.

Hiuan-tsang also tells us that Kucha had her annual car festivals when images of Buddha used to be carried in possession. Thousands of people used to assemble on this occasion. The kings and the nobles had great esteem for Buddhism and the Buddhist teachers. During several days on the occasion of the autumnal equinox every year, the king and all his people, from the highest to the lowest, abstained from public business, observed religious fast and listened to sacred teachings. Even in matter of state affairs, whenever a new decree had to be passed, the king had to take the counsel of the chief priests.

Buddhism continued to flourish in Kucha till the 8th century. Wu-k'ong visited Kucha in 751. He met a Buddhist teacher named Wu-ti-ti-si-yu (Utpal-tsirawne — Skt. Utpalvīrya) living in the Utpal-vihara outside the .western gate of the city. He knew a variety of languages : the languages of India, the countries of Tarim basin and also China. On the request of Wu-K'ong, he translated the *Daśabala-sūtra* and two other works in collaboration with a Khotanese monk, Śīladharma, which are still preserved.

Of the condition of Buddhism in two neighbouring states of Karasahr and Aksu, we know something from the account of Hiuan-tsang. In the 7th century there were about 10 monasteries in Karasahr with 2000 monks, all belonging to the Sarvastivada school of Hinayana. Like the monks of Kucha, they were strict followers of the original rules of Buddhist discipline, and used to read the Sanskrit canonical texts. In Aksu there were also about 10 monasteries with nearly a thousand monks belonging to the Sarvastivada school. It is clear that the monks of these two countries, as well as those of Turfan, in the early period, were dependent on Kucha for leadership in religious matters. Hence there were monasteries in the capital of Kucha specially donated by the rulers of other states for the use of their monks. We have found reference to the monastery in Kucha built by the king of Wen-su (Uch-Turfan). Hiuan-tsang mentions a monastery specially built for the use of Buddhist converts of the country of Turfan.

The Buddhist church of Turfan was dependent on Karasahr and Kucha in the early period, but with the establishment of the Chinese dynasty towards the end of the 5th century, Chinese influences became more and more perceptible. The dynasty, we have seen, reigned till the middle of the 7th century. Buddhism continued to be the religion of the people and the kings even in this period. King Wen-t'ai was on the throne when Hiuan-tsang passed through Turfan in 630. Hiuan-tsang received a warm reception from the king and was accommodated in a monastery near the palace where the pilgrim found a Chinese Buddhist scholar who had studied at Ch'ang-ngan. Wen-t'ai was a fervent Buddhist and would not allow Hiuan-tsang to leave him. He insisted on his staying at Turfan for good. The pilgrim, however, was obdurate in his refusal. Ultimately the king had to yield.

Hiuan-tsang, however, was induced to stay at Turfan for a month and explain the doctrine of the Prajñaparamita. Special arrangement was made for the purpose. "The king prepared large pavilion for the purpose of beginning the religious conferences ; the pavilion could seat three hundred persons or so ; the empress sat on the right of the king, the masters and the chief nobles all took different seats to attend the preaching. Everyday at the time of the preaching, the king himself conducted the master, preceding him with a brazier containing incense. When ascending the pulpit, the king, humbly bowing, placed his footstool and begged him to mount and be seated. Day by day this was done".

When Hiuan-tsang left Turfan, he left with a big caravan supplied by Wen-t'ai. The king, besides, gave him introductory letters to various states and specially to the Ye-hu-Kagan of the Western Turks and to his relative, the Turkish prince who was the master of Tokharestan. The Chinese inscriptions of Turfan of this period contain many references to the influence of Buddhism on the life of the people. Thus an excellent doctor would be mentioned by them as Jivaka — the famous physician mentioned in the Buddhist canon.

Buddhism prospered under the Uigurs. The Turks, we have seen, had become familiar with Buddhism in Tokharestan, and some of the Turkish rulers had shown great leanings towards this religion. The Uigur Turks had inherited that tradition and also imbibed a good deal of this culture from the people of the northern part of the Tarim basin, of Turfan, Karasahr, Kucha and Aksu with whom they were in intimate contact in the 7th century. When they founded the new empire with its headquarters at Turfan in the

9th century, the old civilisation of Kucha-Karasahr had disappeared, but the Uigurs had assimilated much of it with the population. The Uigur empire lasted till the 11th century, and during this long period they developed a new civilisation in which Buddhism had a preponderating place, in spite of the patronage given by some rulers to Manichaeism. A large number of Uigur translations was made from the Tokharian Buddhist texts and that constituted the oldest literature of the Turks.

MUSIC AND ART

Besides Buddhism, Kucha had adopted other elements of Indian culture. The people of Kucha, and also probably their neighbours, were fond of music, and skilled in wind and stringed musical instruments. It is said that the Kuchean musicians were so fond of music that they used to go to the fountains at the time of rainfall and translate the sound of falling waters into music. Fond of music as they were, they could not help borrowing elements of Indian music when they came in contact with India.

We know from the Chinese sources that the names of the seven notes of Kuchean music were :

Ki-che — long tone,
Sha-che — simple and straight tone,
Sha-hou-kia-lan — consonant tone,
Sha-la — consonant and harmonious tone,
Pan-chen — fifth tone,
and Sse-lou-she — tone of the bull.

Of these Sha-che is Sanskrit Ṣaḍja, Sha-hou-kia-lan — Sahagram, Pan-chen — Pañcama and Sse-hou-li-she — Ṛṣabha. Although we cannot identify the remaining names, there is no doubt that the names were borrowed from Sanskrit sources.

Lu-Kuang, after his conquest of Kucha in 383, had taken a Kuchean orchestra party with him to Leang-chou, where the Chinese must have started appreciating this new music. Later on, in the period 550-577, a new party was invited to China by the Wei emperors. The leader of this party was Miao-ta, whose family name was Ts'ao (probably Jhā from Upādhyāya). We are told, in this connection, that Ts'ao was of a Brahmanical family established in Kucha which cultivated music from father to son. In 568, when a Turkish princess was married to a Chinese king, Kuchean musicians came with the princess In this period there were three Kuchean orchestra parties in the Chinese capital, and Kuchean music became extremely popular among the people. An imperial decree tried to stop it, but without success. Even the princes of the imperial family started taking interest in this music.

Kuchean musicians, we are told, were so clever that they could reproduce an air on hearing it only once. The musical parties used to be accompanied by four dancers. One of their favourite demonstrations was the "Dance of the five lions". Each lion was made of 12 men and had a special colour. The demonstration required the assistance of 140 dancers. About the dress and the equipment of the musicians, the Chinese records says : "The musicians use a cap of black cloth. They put on a silken white tunic, a violet-coloured breeches of brocade and a red mantle. The dancers are two in number. They have their hairs plaited and they put on a kaysaa of chao-hia, similar to the dress of the monks. They walk with shoes made of ropes and green hemp. For the music they use the gong, the drum called *kie*, mao-yuan, tu-t'an, the cornet of reed called pi-li, the transversal flute called heng-ti, the sphinx-headed lute called k'ong-hu, the guitar p'i-pa which has five cords, the cymbals and the conch".

A Kuchean musician named Sujīva went to China in the period 560-578. He said that the music which he took to China had seven degrees in the gamut, and that his father, who was famous in the West as a musician, had learnt this music through a tradition transmitted through generations. The music is said to have possessed seven kinds of systems, and the degree in these seven systems had a mysterious concordance. These seven systems seem to have been the Jātis of the Indian music. The Jātis were precursors of the Rāgas, and if we take into account only the seven śuddha notes, their number would be seven.

ANCIENT SITES

The ancient sites in the Turfan oasis are at present Toqsun, Yar, Bazaklik, Murtuq, Sangim, Subashi, Idiqutshahri, Qocho or Qarakhojo and Toyuk. The extensive ruins in those places show that they were very prosperous localities in ancient times. The capital was located at Qarakhojo, 25 miles to the east of present Turfan. Toyuk is a beautiful spot to the Nort-East of Qarakhojo. There are many ruined monastic retreats and shrines in the Toyuk gorge. Cave shrines and temples can be seen on both sides of the gorge for about a mile. Bazaklik is situated in the gorge of a stream which flows towards Qarakhojo and about 2 miles from Murtuk. It contains the largest Buddhist sites of Turfan. There are cave-temples, with wonderful frescoes and numerous Buddhist shrines.

Most of the Buddhist sites in Turfan belong to the Uigur period (750-850) but many a tradition of the earlier Tokharian period must have been inherited by the Uigurs. "Bazaklik stucco figurines or frescoes represent Buddhas of Boddhisattvas which are the final expression in the eastern region, of the Graeco-Buddhist art of Gandhara ; Idiqutshahri frescoes in which we have at times some feminine divinity with Grecian head-dress and lunar divinities of Sangim whose Indian draperies present the happiest combination of Indian suppleness, Hellenic eloquence and Chinese charm."

In Karasahr and Shorchuq sites the remains of a very prosperous Buddhist civilisation have been discovered. The Buddhist art of this region was of mixed origin partly derived from India and partly from Sassanid Iran. On the route to Kucha are the old sites of Yaka-arik, Yangi-hissar and Bugur. This was the historical route connecting Karasahr and Kucha. The ancient sites in Kucha as Kizil, Qumtura, Duldur-Aqur etc. contain the vestiges of the ancient Buddhist art which is also of a mixed character.

CHAPTER V

LANGUAGE AND LITERATURE

STORY OF THE DISCOVERY

We have seen so far that the Chinese History gives us a picture of the ancient states of Eastern Turkestan and a history of their relations with the neighbouring countries from a Chinese angle of vision. The assiduous work of archaeologists have unearthed from the desert sands remnants of ancient art and literature which throw new light on the cultural life of the people mostly from an Indian and partially from local points of view.

The history of this archaeological work is of abiding interest to all students of history. In 1890, a British officer named Col. Bower who was posted at Kucha purchased from the local Turks an extensive birch bark manuscript which was dug out from the sands of Qumtura, a site near Kucha. The manuscript was sent to the Asiatic Society of Bengal and was recognised by Dr. Hoernle to be a Sanskrit medical treatise written in the North Indian script (Gupta) of the 4th century A. D.

A few years later a French traveller Mr. Dutreuil de Rhins brought two birch bark manuscripts from Khotan. They were found on examination to be manuscripts of a new version of Dhammapada in Prakrit, the script being Kharosthi of the 2nd century A. D. similar to that used in the North-Western India under the Kushans. Another part of the manuscript found its way to St. Petersburg (now Leningrad).

These two astounding discoveries drew the attention of the archaeologists all over the world. Deserts of Eastern Turkestan soon become a promising field of antiquarian researches. A Russian Archaeological Mission led by Klementz explored in 1878 the Northern parts of Eastern Turkestan and discovered the remains of ancient civilisation from Idikutshahri, Qocho, Qara-khojo, Turfan, Toyuk and Murtuk in the Turfan oasis.

The Government of India also started taking interest in the work about this time. Dr. (later Sir) Aurel Stein, a trained Archaeologist in the service of the Government and thoroughly acquainted with the routes of North-West frontier was deputed in 1891 to carry on archaeological exploration in the region of Khotan. The results of these investigations were later on published in a volume entitled *Ancient Khotan.*

Stein Mission was followed by three German expeditions under Grünwedel and Von Lecoq between 1903 and 1907. The German archaeologists worked mostly in the Northern part of Eastern Turkestan in Turfan, Kucha, Karasahr, Kizil and Bazaklik. They returned with numerous finds both literary and artistic.

The Government of India sent Stein a second time in 1906 to explore regions beyond Khotan. This time Dr Stein carried his explorations in ancient sites in the southern part of Eastern Turkestan upto the frontier of China. Various sites beyond Khotan in Domoko, Niya, Lou-lan and Miran were excavated and famous Caves of Thousand Buddhas were discovered at Tunhuang. Stein returned in 1908. The result of his investigations in course of his second expedition were later published in the volumes of *Ser-India.*

A French expedition was sent in 1906 under the leadership of the famous Sinologist Paul Pelliot. Pelliot carried on his investigation mostly in the Northern part of Turkestan between 1906 and 1908 in the region of Tumshuk, Kucha and Kizil. He passed most part of his time at Tunhuang studying manuscript collections and the remains of art in the Caves of Thousand Buddhas.

In 1906 and 1908 Russia sent two other missions to Central Asia under the leadership of Beresovsky and Kazaloff. Japan also sent two missions one in 1904 under Count Otani and another a few years later under Tachibana.

The Government of India sent Stein a third time to Central Asia in 1913 for another extensive exploration. Stein returned in 1916 after covering a very wide area including Khotan, Niya, Lou-lan, Tunhuang, Borkul, Guchen, Jimasa, Idikutshahri, Kucha and Aksu. The story of these explorations has been recorded in his volumes on *Innermost Asia.*

The investigations carried on by Stein, Grünwedel, Von Lecoq and Pelliot yielded the most epoch-making results. The collections made by them were properly preserved and placed in the hands of a galaxy of first-rate scholars. The studies of the documents in these collections still continue but the publications made during the last half-a-century have thrown light on numerous aspects of the civilisation of Eastern Asia. These studies have clearly set forth the character of civilisation in Eastern Turkestan during the first millenium of the Christian era. This civilisation although somewhat cosmopolitan is dominated by Indian religion, literature, arts and sciences.

INDIAN SCRIPTS AND LANGUAGES

The literary finds from Central Asia show that Indian scripts were in use for nearly a millenium in the different states of Eastern Turkestan. During the first three centuries of the Christian era Kharosthi script was in use in the Southern states, from Khotan up to Kroraina (Lou-lan) in the Labnor region. Khorosthi as is well known was the common script of North-West India from the time of Asoka up to the end of the Kushan period (third century). It was this script that was carried to the Southern states of Eastern Turkestan by Indian immigrants and was also adopted for official purposes. Khorosthi documents come mostly from the ancient sites of Niya, Endere and Kroraina, and are 782 in number. They are mostly in the form of wooden tablets, leather pieces, silk fragments etc. and throw light on the every day life of the people. They contain a few Buddhist fragementary texts but the character of bulk of the collection is generally profane connected with the political and economic life of the people. The manuscript of Dhammapada discovered by Dutreuil du Rhins, and already referred to is in Khorosthi and belongs to this period.

Kharosthi was supplanted by Brahmi in the 4th Century A. D. and was adopted in the Khotan region as well as in Kucha and Karasahr in the North for literary purposes. In the first stage it is the North Indian Gupta script that was in use in the 4th century. It is used in the Bower Manuscripts, already mentioned, and the fragments of Buddhist texts (specially Vinayapiṭaka) belonging to the Weber collection coming from the Kucha region. An isolated inscription containing the whole text of the

Pratītya-Samutpāda-Sūtra discovered from Tunhuang area is also in this early Brahmi.

Brahmi used in Kucha and Karasahr region during the subsequent centuries is a local adaptation of the early Gupta. Whereas the earlier Gupta has an upright *ductus* the later script is in a slanting style and is usually known to the epigraphists as 'Slanting Gupta.'

'Slanting Gupta' did not come in use in the Khotan region. Two types of modified Gupta scripts were used in this area — one is calligraphic and the other cursive. The calligraphic style was used for literary purposes, specially for copying canonical texts of Buddhism. The cursive style was used in public and private documents as well as in secular literary works.

'Slanting Gupta' used in the North underwent some modifications to adapt itself to use for the local languages. In the Kuchean language and in its allied dialect known as Tokharian, Sanskrit sounds *k t p ś s ṣ n m r l* (क त प श स ष न म र ळ) are somewhat attenuated and hence the corresponding Brahmi signs are underlined in the manuscripts. Modified signs are also used for *w*. No such modification was necessary in the calligraphic and cursive Gupta used in Khotan area as two Khotanese sounds foreign to Sanskrit viz. *ys* and *ṛr* or *rṛ* required no change in the signs.

The documents reveal that apart from local languages which came into literary use later the cultured people of the states of Eastern Turkestan were familiar with two Indian languages, an Indian Prakrit and the Sanskrit. The Prakrit is the language of the Kharosthi documents from Niya, Endere and Kroraina and of the Kharosthi Dhammapada from Khotan. This Prakrit is allied to the spoken language of North-West India in which the Inscriptions of the Kushan period are written. It has some affinities with the literary Prakrit described as Paiśācī by the Prakrit Grammarians. As it was not a sacred language of Buddhism it was not carried to Eastern Turkestan by Buddhist monks but by actual immigrants from the North-West to the Niya-Kroraina region. The language of the documents was the spoken language of the people till the end of the 4th century when the ancient colonies disappeared.

Sanskrit was introduced with Buddhism. Buddhism that was

introduced was of the Sarvāstivāda school of Hinayana which had its stronghold in Kashmir and the North-west. The sacred literature of this school was written in Classical Sanskrit and this was the literature that was studied by the Buddhist scholars of the various states of Eastern Turkestan. Mahayana Buddhism was introduced in the 4th century in Khotan, Kashgar and Kucha. The literature of Mahayana was also in Sanskrit. Medical and astronomical treatises in Sanskrit were also studied by the local scholars.

With the progress of Buddhism in the various states the necessity for translations of sacred texts into local languages was felt. But the local languages thus raised to a literary status were also modelled after Sanskrit not only in their structure but also in the use of vocabulary. The technical terms, religious, philosophical and scientific were largely adapted to the phonetic changes of the local languages.

SANSKRIT CANON

Until the decipherment of the Central Asian documents the Pali Canon was known to be the only authentic sacred literature of Buddhism. There were however the ancient Chinese translations of a complete Tripiṭaka but they were not based on Pali. The original of these translations still remained to be discovered. Central Asian finds came to throw unexpected light on the problem and to establish for the first time that Hinayana Buddhism also possessed a complete Tripiṭaka which is now lost. Central Asian fragments of the canonical texts belong to this Sanskrit Tripiṭaka.

The Sanskrit Tripiṭaka was the Canon of the Sarvāstivāda school and consisted of Sūtrapiṭaka, Vinayapiṭaka and Abhidharmapiṭaka. The Sūtrapiṭaka was a collection of Āgamas roughly corresponding to the five Nikāyas of the Pali Suttapiṭaka, with the difference that there were four Āgamas in Sanskrit whereas Pali has five Nikāyas.

The four Āgamas called Dīrgha, Madhyama, Saṁyukta and Ekottara were translated into Chinese at different dates between the 4th and 6th centuries. The Dīrgha-Āgama was translated by Buddhayaśas in 412-413, the Madhyamāgama in 397-398 by Gautama Saṅghadeva ; Saṁyuktāgama in 420-427 by Guṇabhadra and Ekottarāgama by Dharmanandi in 384-385. All the translators hailed from Kashmir. This shows that the collections had been completed in Kashmir before the 4th century, were widely studied there and were carried to Central Asia and China along with Sarvāstivāda Buddhism towards the end of the 4th century. The writing of the Central Asian manuscripts belong to the same period.

Of the *Sūtrapiṭaka* we now possess fragments of Sūtras of at least three Āgamas. They are the following :

Dīrghāgama — (1) *Saṁgīti-sūtra* — the fragment contains an enumeration of different dharmas into ten classes according to the number of items constituting such dharmas. There is a *Saṁgīti-suttanta* in Pali Dīgha-nikāya but the Sanskrit text agrees more with *Saṁgīti-sūtra* of the Dīrghāgama in Chinese translation (2) *Āṭa-nāṭiya-Sūtra* — it is very different from the Pali *Āṭanātiya-suttanta* but a similar text under the title *Mahāsamaya-sūtra* is found in Chinese Dīrghāgama. The *Āṭanātiya-sūtra* may be a later-elaboration of this text.

Madhyamāgama — (1) *Upāli-sūtra*, — which is different from the corresponding Pali text (Majjhima 56) but agrees with the Chinese translation (Madhyamāgama 133). (2) *Śuka-Sūtra*, a text dealing with the doctrine of Karma and retribution. The Pali text (*Majjhima* 135) has a different title — *Culla Kamma-vibhaṅga* which is more elaborate. The fragment agrees with the corresponding text in Chinese Madhyamāgama (text No. 170). The text was very popular in Central Asia and China as shown by its translation in the language of Kucha and four separate Chinese translations which still exist.

Saṁyuktāgama — (1) *Pravāraṇa-sūtra* — the fragment of the Sanskrit text agrees with the Chinese translations of Guṇavarman. There are two other separate Chinese translations of the text, one by Dharma kṣema made in 266-317 A. D. and the other by Fa-hien (Dharmabhadra) in the 10th century. The text has some general agreement with Pali *Vaṅgīsa-thera-saṁyutta* of the Saṁyutta-nikāya.

(2) *Candropama sūtra* — the fragment has a general agreement with Pali Saṁyutta (third sutta of the Kassapa section) but agrees more closely with the Chinese translation. (3) *Śakti-sūtra* corresponds to Pali *Satti-sutta* of the *Opamma* section of Saṁyutta-nikāya. There is a later Chinese translation of the text. (4) *Nidāna-sūtra* dealing with the chain of causation and with the means of its destruction — corresponding with Pali Nidāna-saṁyutta of the Saṁyutta-nikāya (XIII, 15), also found in the Chinese translation of the Saṁyuktāgama. There are also independent Chinese translations of the text. (5) *Kokanada sūtra* (= Chinese translation of the Saṁyukta 34, Pali Aṅguttara 196-198). (6) *Anāthapiṇḍada-sūtra* (Saṁyukta 34, Pali Aṅg. V 185-189), (7) *Dīrghanakha-sūtra* (Saṁyukta 34-35, Pali Majjhima 487-501) (8) *Śarabha-sūtra* (Saṁyukta 35, Pali Aṅg. I 185-188) (9) *Parivrājaka-sthavira-sūtra* (Saṁyukta 35), (10) *Brāhmaṇa-satyāṁsūtra* (Samyukta 35).

The *Vinaya Piṭaka* of the Sarvāstivāda school is well represented by the fragment of texts coming from the Northern part of Eastern Turkestan. Like other sections of the canonical literature of the school the Vinayapiṭaka was written in Sanskrit. A complete text of the *Prātimokṣa-sūtra* belonging Sarvāstivāda Vinaya was discovered by the French Mission in the ruins of Duldur-Aqur at Kucha. The text contains all the sections such as Nidāna, Pārājika, Saṅghādiśeṣa, etc. The Pali Pāṭimokkha corresponds in major part with the text. It agrees literally with the Chinese translation made by Kumarjıva in 404 A. D. *Bhikṣuṇīprātimokṣa* of the school is represented by fragments discovered in the Kucha region by both French and German missions.

Besides a very important text entitled *Mahāparinirvāṇasūtra* belonging to the Mūlasarvāstivāda-Vinaya which also wrote in Sanskrit has been restored from a number of fragments discovered by the German mission from the ruins of Sorcuq near Turfan and of Tumshuq near Maral-bashi. Parallel texts were also discovered from the ruins of Kizil near Kucha. Mūlasarvāstivāda school was developed from the Sarvāstivāda and flourished in Kashmir. It possessed an extensive Vinayapiṭaka in Sanskrit but it was known for many years only from the Chinese and Tibetan translations and a number of fragments contained in the Nepalese text called *Divyāvadāna* A considerable portion of the original text has now been restored from manuscripts discovered in a ruined monastery in Gilgit by Sir Aurel Stein. The *Mahāparinirvāṇa-sūtra* from Eastern Turkestan belongs to this Vinaya collection and agrees with the Mahāvagga of the Pali Vinayapiṭaka.

The *Abhidharmapiṭaka* of the Sarvāstivāda school was also known and studied in Central Asia. This piṭaka consists of seven texts which are preserved in Chinese translations but a fragment of the original Sanskrit text of the *Sangītiparyāya* has been discovered from the caves of Bamiyan in Afganistan. The script is "Slanting Gupta" which was in use in the Northern part of Eastern Turkestan.

Fragments of a few sūtras which belong to the Sūtrapiṭaka of Hinayāna but not strictly included in any of the Āgamas have also been identified : *Daśabalasūtra*, *Mahāvadānasūtra*, *Saptabuddhaka* etc. The *Daśabalasūtra* was a very popular text. It agrees partially with Pali *Dasakanipāta* of the Aṅguttara-nikāya and the *Daśaka* section of Chinese translation of Ekottarāgama. There is also a separate Chinese translation which was made in Kucha towards the end of the 8th century by the Chinese envoy Wu-K'ong in collaboration with a Kuchean monk named W-ti-ti-si-yu.

Mahayāna canon was also studied in Central Asia. Fragments of a few important texts amply prove this. There are fragments of : (1) *Vajracchedikā* belonging to the Prajñāpāramitā class, (2) *Ratnarāsi-sūtra* of the Ratnakūṭa class, (3) *Ratnadhvaja*, Candragarbha and Candrapāla sūtras of the Mahāsannipāta class, and (4) *Mahāparinirvāṇa-sūtra* of the Nirvāṇa class. We have besides fragments of two other major texts of Mahayāna, viz. — this *Saddharmapuṇḍarīka-sūtra* and *Suvarṇaprabhāsottama-sūtra*. Texts on dhāraṇis or magical formulae belonging to later Mahayāna, have also been found e. g. *Anantamukha-dhāraṇi*, *Suraṁgamasamādhi* and *Sītāta-patradhāraṇī*.

DHAMMAPADA AND UDANAVARGA

Dhammapada in Pali is a unique text consisting of very old verses many of which are found in different parts of the canon. The verses were arranged in sections and put in the form of present compilation later by an author whose name is lost. Besides the Pali Dhammapada we are now in possession of two other similar collections from amongst the Central Asian finds. One of them is the Dhammapada in Prakrit and the other is the Udānavarga in Sanskrit.

We have already referred to the discovery of the text of Prakrit Dhammapada from the region of Khotan. The text is written in Kharosthi script of about the 3rd century. The language is different from Pali and is a Middle Indo-Aryan which is akin to the dialect spoken in the North-Western India in the Kushan period or in the period immediately preceding. The text is fragmentary and some verses from the sections entilted Apramāda, Cita, Puṣa, Sahasa, Panita, Bala, Jarā and Suha have come down to us. A clear idea of the difference in language may be formed from the following verses :

Prakrit

अप्रमदु अमुतपद प्रमदु मुचुनो पद ।
अप्रमत न मियन्ति य प्रमत यधा मुतु ॥

Pali

अप्पमादो अमतपदम् पमादो मुच्चुनो पदम् ।
अप्पमत्ता न मियन्ति ये प्रमत्ता यथा मता ॥

Sanskrit

अप्रमादो ह्यमृतपदं प्रमादो मृत्युनः पदम् ।
अप्रमत्ता न म्रियन्ते ये प्रमत्ताः सदा मृताः ॥

The Pali Dhammapada belonged to the Theravāda school. The Prakrit Dhammapada must have belonged to a school which wrote in Prakrit.

Stein, Grünwedel and Pelliot missions brought from Central Asia fragments of manuscripts of a Sanskrit text called Udānavarga. The Grünwedel and Pelliot Manuscripts are almost complete. Fragments from Stein collection were published by La Vallée Poussin (J. R. A. S. 1912. 356-377). The complete section of *Yugavarga* was edited from three manuscripts of the German collection by Pischal under the title Turfan recension of Dhammapada. Lévi edited the first section, *Apramādavarga* from the French and published into (J. As. 1912). The whole text of the Pelliot Manuscript was later edited and published bp Dr. N. P. Chakravarti.

The text of the Udānavarga, written in Sanskrit is a collection akin to the Dhammapada, in some places more extensive. The collection is attributed to Dharmatrāta, a famous teacher of the Sarvāstivāda school who was contemporaneous with Kanishka, and lived in the first century. The Tibetan translation under the name Udānavarga had been rendered into English by Rockhill.

Dhammapada texts in their various recensions were very popular in Central Asia and China. Besides the two texts already mentioned translations in local languages had also been made and were widely read. There are four separate Chinese translations, based on four different recensions of the text, three of which had been carried from Central Asia to China. They are (i) *Fa-kiu king*—Dharmapadasūtra translated in 224 A. D. ; (ii) *Fa-k'iu-p'i yu king*—Dharmapada-avadāna sūtra translated between 290 and 306 A. D. ; (iii) *Chu yao king* translated in 398-399 A. D. The last named text is the translation of the Udānavarga. The first two translations were probably based on a text similar to that of the Prākrit Dhammapada.

POETICAL WORKS — ASVAGHOSA & MATRCETA

Remains of the works of the two great Buddhist poets Aśvaghoṣa and Mātṛceṭa were discovered amongst the Central Asian finds. Fragments of the works of Aśvaghoṣa were brought by the German mission from Turfan region. Aśvaghoṣa as is well known was a contemporary of King Kanishka and a philosopher, poet and dramatist of the first order. Two of his poetical works, *Buddha-carita*, and *Saundarānanda* are known in original and a third, the

Sūtrālaṁkāra is preserved in Chinese translation of Kumārajīva. Besides a philosophical work entitled *Śradhotpāda-śāstra* has also been preserved in Chinese translation which is widely studied in China and Japan.

Central Asian remains throw more light on his other works. A fragment of the *Buddhacarita* brought from Turfan region shows that the text was studied by the Buddhist monks of Central Asia. A drama entitled *Śāriputra-prakaraṇa* discovered in the same region and not known from other sources is ascribed to Aśvaghoṣa. Only portions of the original work have been found, but they clearly show that it was a remarkable work. It is the oldest Indian drama known to us and presupposes a great development in the dramatic art. The work is in Sanskrit but there are dialogues, in Prakrits which are older than the dramatic Prakrits used in classical Sanskrit dramas.

Another work of controversial authorship was also discovered by the German mission in Turfan region. It is a poetical work in Sanskrit which agrees with the *Sūtrālaṃkāra* of Aśvaghoṣa as known from the Chinese translation of the work by Kumārajīva. But the colophons of the Turfan manuscript ascribe the work to Kumāralāta. The colophon runs thus : *iti ārya Kumāralātāyāṁ Kalpanālaṁkṛtāyām dṛṣṭāntapaṅktyāṃ.* We have sometimes the word *Kalpanāmaṇḍitikāyāṃ* instead of *Kalpanālaṃkṛtāyāṃ*. Kumāralāta, in one context is described as a Bhikṣu of Takṣaśila (Taxila).

Prof. Lüders who deciphered the manuscript, edited and published it was of opinion that the name of the work was *Kalpanāmaṇḍitikā* and that its author was Kumāralāta. The Chinese tradition ascribed the work to Aśvaghoṣa through mistake.

Kumāralāta was of course a well-known Buddhist scholar of Taxila. His name is transcribed in Chinese as Ku-mo-lo-lo-to and translated as *tong-shou* "boy-received". The Tibetan tradition says that he belonged to the Sautrāntika school. The Buddhist tradition further records that he was 'the Sun shining in the North while Aśvaghoṣa illuminated the East, Nāgārjuna the West and Āryadeva the South' Kumāralāta's fame was so great that he was taken by force to the country of Kie-pan-to i. e. Tashkurghan

(see ante p. 43) in the Pamir. He is said to have composed many śāstras but none has come down to us either in original or in translation. The Turfan manuscript however attributes the present work to him.

Kumāralāta is described in Chinese tradition as a "Master of comparisons" (*dṛṣṭānta*) and as founder of a "school of comparisons" (Dārṣṭāntika) which was a branch of the Sautrāntika school. The principal work of Kumāralāta is mentioned in the Chinese texts as *Yu man lun—Dṛṣṭānta-mālā (-paṅkti)-śāstra.* On these grounds Lévi has expressed the opinion that the name of the Turfan text was really *Dṛṣṭāntapaṅkti* (as found in the colophon) and that *Kalpanāmaṇḍitikā* is an adjective to it. The Turfan text is considered by Lévi to be a new edition of the Sūtrālaṁkāra of Aśvaghoṣa expanded by the addition of moral lessons and apologues in the form of examples (*dṛṣṭānta*) according to the practice of the Dārṣṭāntika school. The Turfan text therefore represents partially the Sūtrālaṃkāra of Aśvaghoṣa.

The Hymns of Mātṛceṭa : The fragments of the poems of another poet of great fame have been brought to light both in Sanskrit original and Tokharian translation. The poet was Mātṛceṭa who is well known from Tibetan and Chinese translations. A full account of the poet and his works is given by Yi-tsing (Takakusu — *Buddhist Practices in India* pp. 156ff). "In India" he says, "numerous hymns of praise to be sung at worship have been most carefully handed down, for every talented man of letters has praised in verse whatsoever person he deemed most worthy of worship. Such a man was the venerable Mātṛceṭa, who by his great literary talent and virtues, excelled all learned men of his age. The following story is told of him : While the Buddha was living, he was once, while instructing his followers wandering in a wood among the people. A nightingale in the wood, seeing the Buddha, majestic as a gold mountain, adorned by his perfect signs, began to utter its melodious notes, as if it sang in praise of him. The Buddha, looking back to his disciples, said : 'The bird transported with joy at sight of me, unconsciously utters its melodious notes. On account of this good deed, after my departure (Nirvāṇa) this bird shall be born in human form, and named Mātṛceṭa, and he shall praise my virtues with true appreciation. Previously as a follower of another religion, when born as man, Mātṛceṭa had been an ascetic, and had worshipped Maheśvaradeva. When a worshipper of this deity, he had composed hymns in his praise. But on becoming acquainted with the fact that his birth had been foretold, he became a convert to Buddhism, robed in colour and free from worldly cares. He mostly engaged himself in praising and glorifying the Buddha, repented of his past sins, and was desirous henceforward of Buddha's good example regretting that he could not see the Great Teacher himself but his image only. In fulfilment of the above prediction he wrote hymns in praise of the Buddha's virtues to the greatest extent of his literary powers.

"He composed first a hymn consisting of four hundred ślokas, and afterwards another of one hnndred and fifty. He treats generally of the Six Pāramitās and expounds all the excellent qualities of the Buddha, the World-honoured One. These charming compositions are equal in beauty to the heavenly flowers, and the high principles which they contain rival in dignity the lofty peaks of a mountain. Consequently in India all who compose hymns imitate his style, considering him the father of literature. Even men like the Bodhisattvas Asaṅga and Vasubandhu admired him greatly. Throughout India every one who becomes a monk is taught Mātṛceṭa's two hymns as soon as he can recite the five and ten precepts".

Of the two works of Mātṛceṭa, Yi-tsing while in Nalanda translated one in 150 verses into Chinese. It was revised by him later on in China (708). The Chinese catalogues render the title as *Sārdhaśataka-Buddhapraśaṁsāgāthā* but the original Sanskrit title is now known as *Śatpañcaśatikā-stotra*.

As the colophon of the Tibetan translation of the *Śatpañcaśatikā-stotra* attributes the work to Aśvaghoṣa and as Taranath also takes him to be identical with Aśvaghoṣa Mātṛceṭa has been considered to be another name of Aśvaghoṣa. In any way Mātṛceṭa was also a contemporary of Kanishka, and if not identical with Aśvaghoṣa, was just his elder contemporary and lived in the first century A. D.

The tradition which Yi-tsing records about teaching the Hymns of Mātṛceṭa to all monks is probably very old. That is the reason for which the hymns seem to have been very popular in Central Asia too. Manuscripts of the Sanskrit original of the *Śatpañcaśatika-stotra* have been brought from various sites in Central Asia such as Jigdalik-Bai, Tunhuang and Khora. Tokharian translations of the text have also been brought by the German expedition from Turfan.

The various fragments of Sanskrit manuscript have brought to light the following verses: 23-38, 48-74, 117-131 and 146-150 (Hoernle pp. 58ff.). Fragments of verses 147-150 were also discovered in a leaf in the Pelliot Collection (Lévi, J. As. 1910, p. 450). Two verses may be quoted here as examples of the composition of Mātṛceṭa —

विमिश्रात् सारमेवापि निर्दोषम् मनसाहृतम्
क्षणे सूक्तम् दुरुक्तम् तु विषवत् परिवर्जितम् ।
क्रीणता रत्नसारज्ञः प्राणैरपि सुभाषितम्
पराक्रम्यत बोध्यर्थं तासु तासु हि जातिषु ।

"From the mingled, only the faultless essence was taken into the mind at once, the well-said : but the ill-said like poison was avoided.

By thee oh knower of the world of jewels, purchasing with life what was well-said, heroism was shown for the sake of bodhi in a variety of births."

Fragments of the other work of Mātṛecṭa, the *Catuḥśataka-stotra* also have been discovered from Central Asia. There is no Chinese translation of the text but the Tibetan translation gives the name of the work as *Varṇanārha-varṇanāstotra.* Fragments of Sanskrit manuscript were discovered from Khora (near Karasahr) and Jigdalik (near Bai). Only thirty-two verses have been discovered from the fragments and it appears from them that the text was divided into 12 chapters. We have all verses of Chap. I, 9 of Chap. VI, 2 of Chap. VII and 10 of Chap. XII. The colophon of the chapters give the full title of the work as *Varṇanārha-varṇe Buddhastotre Catuḥśatakam.*

The literary value of the verses is as great as that of the other work :

अह्रो संसारदौरात्म्यम् अह्रो निर्वाणसन्तता
नाथोऽपि सन् तत्र गत करुणात्मा त्वया सदृक्
नानागतभयम् नोक्तम् न नेत्री न प्रवर्तिता ।
न संसारश्च गमितो नाभयत्वम् चतुर्विधः ।

(7) Ah, the misery of Saṃsāra ! Ah, the peace of Nirvāṇa though he is a lord, he went there (i. e. into Saṃsāra), having a soul of pity like thine.

(8) Future fears were certainly told, guidance was certainly prompted : mundane existence of four kinds was certainly made to attain fearlessness.

SANSKRIT MEDICAL TEXTS

Buddhist missionaries had carried to Central Asia not only Indian religion and literature but also scientific knowledge. We have indirect evidences of the use of Indian astronomy and mathematics ; but no manuscripts of astronomical and mathematical texts have been so far discovered. The literary remains brought from the ancient sites however contain a large number of fragments of Sanskrit medical texts which were used in Central Asia from the 4th to about the 8th century A. D.

Col. Bower discovered three different medical texts from an old stupa near Kucha. They are usually known as Bower Manuscripts One of these texts deals with garlic, its origin and use. The author says that garlic is able to cure many diseases and can extend the life up to 100 years. The text also deals with digestion, an elixir for life of 1000 years, correct mixing of ingredients, other medicines, lotion and ointment for eyes etc. The second text contains 14 medical formulae for external and internal use. The third text which is the largest portion of the collection is called *Navanītaka*, "cream" and contains an abstract of the earlier medical literature. It deals with the preparation of powder, decoctions, oils, and also with injections, elixirs, aphrodisiacs, nursing of children etc. The earlier literature quoted in the text includes: Agniveśa, Bheḍa, Hārita, Jātukarṇa, Ksārapāṇi Parāśara and Suśruta.

Besides the Sanskrit original of medical texts there are other evidences to show that Indian medical literature was widely used in Central Asia. We know from translations of Indian texts into Kuchean and Khotanese languages that the knowledge of Indian medicine was very wide-spread. These translations clearly bear out that even the local doctors who did not know Sanskrit were making use of the Indian system.

LOCAL TRANSLATIONS

We have already spoken about the Kuchean and Tokharian languages before (ante pp. 68 ff. and p. 28 ff.). The language of Kucha which was known to the Uigur-Turks under the name *Küsana* was spoken in the entire region from Aksu (ancient Bharuka) to Turfan (ancient Agnideśa). Literary remains in this language have been discoverd from different parts of this region mainly by the French archaeological mission. A few fragments also belong to the Stein collection and a few others were found also among the German and Russian collections. The fragments of Kuchean texts of the Stein and Russian collections were studied and published along with the French collection by Sylvain Lévi and later by Jean Filliozat (*Textes Koutchéens*; *Fragments de Textes Koutchéens de Médicine et de Magie*). Kuchean texts of the German collection were never published.

The fragments of texts in the other dialect which has been called Tokharian were discovered by the German mission in Karasahr and Turfan region. The spoken language of the area however, we have seen, was Kuchean. The mural inscriptions in the Buddhist caves in this area are also written in Kuchean. Tokharian literature in all likelihood was developed in some other area, probably in Tokharestan and the texts had been brought to this region during the Uigur period. The German collection of 417 fragments were edited by Sieg and Siegling and published with plates in a volume entitled *Tocharische Sprachreste*. Among the fragments the major part (383) comes from Shorchuk in Karasahr and the rest from the sites of Bazaklik, Murtuq, Sangim and Idikutshahri at Turfan.

Kuchean and Tokharian fragments are all translations of Sanskrit Buddhist texts and contain some bilingual pieces with original Sanskrit by the side of translations. These bilingual pieces were of great help in the interpretation of the language. The Kuchean fragments have beeen fully studied and identified. We have fragments of the Kuchean translation of Sarvāstivāda-Vinaya such as *Prātimokṣa*, *Prāyaścittika*, and *Pratideśanīya*. These canonical rules of monastic discipline were of constant use to the Buddhist communities in Central Asia and required translations in local languages so that monks not well versed in Sanskrit could understand their implications. The bilingual texts must also have been used as handbooks for teaching Sanskrit to the local Buddhists. We have besides Kuchean translations of *Udānavarga*, *Udānastotra* and *Udānālaṁkāra* which were very popular with the Buddhists. There are also fragments of Kuchean translation of a very extensive Sanskrit work entitled *Karmavibhaṅga*, a text on the retribution of acts (*Karma*) which was used by the Buddhist priests as a handy text illustrative of the doctrine of transmigration.

Kuchean translations of medical and Tantrik texts have also been studied, identified and published. We have already mentioned the translations of a medical text entitled *Yogaśataka*. It is a work in about one hundred verses attributed sometimes to Nāgārjuna and sometimes to Vararuci. The original Sanskrit text is known through Nepalese and other manuscripts and also through a Tibetan translation. The *Yogaśataka* was an excellent abridgement of standard Sanskrit medical texts and a convenient handbook used by medical practitioners in India and abroad. We have besides a number of fragments of Kuchean translation of medical texts from Pelliot, Stein and Weber collections. These have not been identified on account of their fragmentary character but comparison with such medical texts as Caraka and Suśruta shows that they were based on standard Indian texts. Sanskrit names of drugs are not translated but transliterated with phonetic changes necessary for their adoption in local language ; examples arīrak (harītakī), kurkam (kurkuma), akaru (aguru), aśvakanta (aśvagandhā), apamārka (apāmārga) etc.

Fragments of translations of Buddhist texts in the other dialect called Tokharian, although published have not been closely studied. They contain bilingual texts and have amongst them such popular texts as the Udānavarga.

Ancient Khotanese known through the translations of Buddhist texts was at first described as 'North-Aryan,' and subsequently as Śaka language. Although the name 'North-Aryan' has been totally discarded some scholars still persist in retaining the name Śaka. Whether it was exclusively a language spoken by the Śakas still remains to be determined. As the Khotanese presented by the translations is found for the first time in a late form in documents of the 7th-8th centuries when Śakas were practically forgotten, it is safer to describe the language as we have done before as Eastern Iranian dialect.

Khotanese translations belong to a late period when Hinayana Buddhism had practically disappeared from the Khotan region and Mahayana had become the predominant religion. The translations therefore are mostly of Mahayana texts. We have so far fragments of the translations of the *Suvarṇaprabhāsa-sūtra*, *Vajracchedikā*, *Aparimitāyus-sūtra*, *Bhadracaryādeśanā*, *Jātakastava* and *Maitreya-Samiti-nāṭaka*.

Khotanese translations of two Indian medical texts also have been found. These are the *Siddhasāra* and *Jīvakapustaka*. The *Siddhasāra* is attributed to one Ravigupta. The Khotanese rendering was based on the Tibetan translation. The fragment contains portions of the following chapters : *tantra*, *dravya*, *arśa*, *bhagandara*, *pāṇḍuroga*, *mūtrakṛccha*, *udāvarta*, *netra-roga* etc. The original of the other text, the *Jīvakapustaka* has not been traced but the interlinear Sanskrit verses show that it was Sanskrit.

Sogdian language, we have seen (ante p. 38) was spoken not only in ancient Sogdiana but also in other parts of Eastern Turkestan where colonies of Sogdian merchants had been established. It might have been, as suggested by Pelliot, a sort of *lingua franca* in Central Asia. It was used by Manichaean priests in the Uigur period in the 9th and 10th centuries A. D. but earlier it was used also by the Buddhist priests. A few Sogdian translations of Buddhist texts have been discovered. These are the *Dīrghanakha-sūtra, Vessāntara-Jātaka, Vimalakīrti-nirdeśa, Dhyānasūtra, Dhūta-sūtra, Nīlakaṇṭha-dhāraṇī* and *Padmacintāmaṇi-dhāraṇi-sūtra.*

With the establishment of Uigur Empire with its capital in Turfan region in the 9th century Buddhism found yet another patron in the Turks. They assimilated the entire Buddhist culture prevalent in Central Asia from the Oxus valley up to Karasahr, with its literature, religion and art. Tokharian Buddhist texts were translated into Turkish. We have thus translations of *Maitreyasamiti-nāṭaka, Suvarṇaprabhāsa-sūtra, Jātakas, Sūtra of Kalyānaṁkara and Pāpaṁkara* etc. Although we have a few Turkish documents in Brahmi, knowledge of Sanskrit was almost obsolete. A new epoch of Buddhim had started and India did not play any direct part in its transmission,

NEW ASPECTS

Buddhist Literature in course of its migration from India to China assumed new aspects in central Asia. The famous monasteries of Central Asia became active centres not only for the preservation and propagation of the canon but also for its reconstitution. In course of their literary activities conscious efforts were made by the monks to naturalise the canon by introducing in it such elements as would make it a Ser-Indian literature as well. Pseudo-canonical Mahayana literature was also created in different parts of the country.

Chinese evidences dating from the middle of the sixth century tell us that the country of Cokkuka near Khotan (ante p. 48) was a great centre of Mahayana Buddhism. The king of the country was also devoted to this faith. When monks from other countries came to Cokkuka they were first to submit to an examination. If they were found to be followers of Hinayana they were sent back. If they were found to be Mahayanist they were invited to stay. In the palace of the king there were three copies of the great Sūtras. *Mahaprajñāpāramitā, Mahāsannipāta,* and *Avataṁsaka.* The king himself was their custodian and kept the keys of the chamber where they were stored. He opened the doors everytime they were to be taken out for reading and then kept them safely back. Other Sūtras were jealously guarded in a precipitious mountain in the neighbourhood of Cokkuka. The following Sūtras, all Mahayana were kept there : *Mahāsannipāta, Avataṁsaka, Vaipulya, Ratnakūṭa, Laṅkāvatāra, Śāriputra-dhārani, Mahaprajñāpāramita, Aṣṭasāhasrika-Prajñāpāramitā*, and *Mahāmegha.*

The canonical Sūtras mentioned above were no doubt of Indian origin but an analysis of some of them from their ancient Chinese translations clearly show that they were naturalised in Ser-India. The *Sūryagarbha* and the *Candragarbha* are two important Sūtras of the Mahāsannipāta collection. They are preserved in Chinese translation of about the middle of the sixth century by Narendrayaśas. The Sanskrit original of the texts is now lost.

The *Sūryagarbha-sūtra* in one of its sections mentions Buddhist holy places. In this list we have besides the holy places in India. Cīnasthāna (China), Khasa (Kashgar ?) and Gomasālagandha Caitya on the Gośṛṅga mountain of Khotan. It was according to the text one of the holiest places visited by myriads of Buddhist devotees. We already know that Gomasālagandha was a historical place in Khotan (ante p. 53).

The *Candragarbha-sūtra* contains two lists of places hallowed by Buddha. In the first list we have mention of 53 kingdoms amongst which the following belong to the Ser-Indian region : Aśkoka, Darada, Khasa, Cokkuka, Sha-lei (Kashgar). Khotan, Kucha, Bharuka, Hecyuka, Yi-ni (Agnideśa ?), Shan-Shan (Kroraina) and Cīnasthāna. In the second list we have enumeration of the number of incarnations of Buddha in various countries. In countries outside India, Śulika (Sogdiana) had 28, Po-sse (Persia) 20, Khasa 28, Cokkuka 20, Khotan 180, Kucha 99, Bharuka 24, Hecyuka 18, Yi-ni (Agni ?) 80, Shan-Shan (Kroraina) 29 and Cīnasthāna 255. Judging by the number of incarnations, Khotan, Kucha and China are given places of the greatest honour in the Buddhist world.

The Chinese sources contain the story of the tragic death of an Indian Buddhist scholar Dharmakṣema during his journey to Khotan in order to get complete canonical texts. Dharmakṣema belonged to Central India and was a follower of Mahayana. He had found in his own country only ten chapters of the famous Mahayana text the *Mahāparinirvāṇa-sūtra.* On getting the information that the rest of the text was to be found in Kashmir he went to Kashmir but in vain. He then went over to China and settled in Leang-chou where he translated Buddist texts at the request of the local ruler during 413-433 A. D. While translating his copy of the *Mahāparinivāṇa-sūtra* he got the information that the complete text could be found in Khotan. He then went to Khotan where he discovered a second part of the text which he brought back to Leang-chou and translated. The text still appeared to him to be incomplete. On getting further information that there was a last part of the text in Khotan he immediately started for Khotan but was murdered on the way. It is clear from the account that the original Indian text was being amplified in Khotan in the 5th century.

"The Tale of Wise Man and the Fool" was a Buddhist text of great popularity in the Ser-Indian region. It is now known through Chinese, Tibetan and Mongolian translations. Fragment of a Kuchean translation in also known. Although the story is similar to the *Prabhāsāvadāna* of the Avadānakalpalatā it is doubtful if the text had an Indian original. We know on the contrary that the original was collected from Khotan. An account appended to Chinese translation of 445 A. D. tells us that eight Chinese monks headed by Hui Kio went to the west in search of Sanskrit texts. They came to Khotan and put up in the Mahāvihāra. The *Pañcavārṣika-pariṣad* was on at that time. Teachers versed in the Tripiṭaka were engaged in giving daily explanations of the holy texts. The Chinese monks attended the lectures and applied themselves to acquire a knowledge of the foreign language. They took down notes of what they heard in course of the lectures. On getting back to Turfan they reassembled their notes and made a book of it. They thought it was an Avadāna and gave it a new title *Hien Yu King*—the Sūtra of the Wise and the Fool.

A Buddhist scholar of Kucha named Li-yen compiled in the 7th century a Sanskrit Chinese lexicon which has been preserved in the

Chinese Tripiṭaka. Although the lexicon was modelled after Sanskrit *Kośas* it contains words of Central Asian origin such as *kalama* (pen), *kakari* (paper), *makara* (monkey) *kavaṣi* (sandal) and names of places in Central Asia and China such as Truṣaka (Turk), Korttana (Khotan), Kucina (Kucha), Wu, & Shu (Provinces of China) Kumudana (Khumdan, i. e. Ch'ang-ngan, capital of China).

Intercourse between India, and the Central Asian kingdoms and China had necessitated the compilation not only of bi-lingual lexicons but also of conversational primers. The text of such a primer has come down to us. It is a Sanskrit-Khotanese text. Sanskrit is corrupt and much influenced by Khotanese pronunciation. We quote below from the Sanskrit text only as it clearly sets forth how the bi-lingual need was being fulfilled. This is a conversation between an Indian Bhikṣu and a man of Kan-chou (Western China). The Bhikṣu was going on a pilgrimage to Wu-tai Shan, the lgendary abode of Mañjuśrī.

Śāṃbanā svastī kuśalaśariri
ttava prrasadaina kuśala—
ttava śāṃbana asti
Kaśmīṁ sthane agatta
Gaustana-deśa-agatta—
Hīduka-deśe kī-kale agatta
Saṁbatsara-dvaya babūva
Gaṁstana-deśai kūtra sthanai ttaiṣṭatta
Sagaramai ttaiṣtatta.
Kasmi Sagaramai
Rajsa Sāmbana drraiṣṭa
Śāṃbana drraiṣṭa
idanī kūtra gatsasi
China daise gatsāmi

"Are you well or not, at ease ?
By your favour I am well
Is it well with you or not ?
Whence have you come ?

I have come from Khotan.
When did you come from India ?
Two years ago.
Where did you stay in Khotan ?
I stayed in a Saṅghārāma.
In which Saṅghārāma did you stay ?
Did you duly see the King or not ?
I duly saw him.
Now where are you going ?
I am going to China."

APPENDIX

I

ROLE OF CENTRAL ASIAN NOMADS IN INDIAN HISTORY

I am grateful to you for the honour you have done me by asking me to preside over this august assembly. The responsibility that you have assigned to me is indeed very great and I am afraid I am not the person who can discharge it to your satisfaction. It seems that the most difficult task of a President is to choose the subject of his address. I have failed to discover a strict principle that might guide us in this matter and make our task easier. The two alternatives before us, I believe, are either to give a survey of the work done in our field of study since we last met or to deal with a particular problem that would interest every one of us. A survey without a proper consideration of the values will be a simple catalogue of works that are more or less known to us. An evalution of the merits and demerits of such works again is beset with difficulties of which we are all aware. I shall therefore choose the other alternative and discuss some problems of the ancient history of India which, although studied on numerous occasions for more than half a century, have not yet lost their interest to us. I am however fully conscious of my shortcomings and I hope you will be indulgent towards me if I ill fulfil my task.

The problems to which I should like to draw your attention are connected with the role of the Central Asian nomads in the history of India. While dealing with these invaders we have been in the habit of attaching greater importance to the foreign sources of information than to our own literature. I do not however deny that for nearly one thousand years, from the end of the second century before Christ upto the eighth, the Chinese sources supply us with more definite information on the movements of the Central Asian nomads than any other source but there is no reason for attaching greater importance to the Greek and Latin texts than to our own for their early history. In fact the classical writers derived their knowledge of these people either from the Persians or from the Indians. The recent researches into the Central Asian antiquities have shown that the ancient Indians possessed a fairly precise knowledge of these people.

The region beyond the Himalayas was never so isolated from India as we often think. The people of Northern India and specially the people of the Punjab possessed some knowledge of this region and were in contact with the nomads almost in every age. They did not consider them foreigners as we do now, simply because the distinction between them, both physical and cultural were not so great as to create a sharp difference between them. Conflict arose only in cases when the newcomers tried to unsettle the established political conditions but peaceful infiltration was generally a welcome feature as it contributed to the prosperity of the country and proved an added military strength to the local rulers. The Brahmanical social code always provided them with an independent place in the society. Although it meant the formation of new castes it did not hurt their *amour-propre* but made them willing partners of an ever-growing civilisation.

As early as the later Vedic period the Indian writers show an acquaintance with the people beyond the northern and north-western frontiers. In the *Atharvaveda* (V. 22, 5-9) the fever *takman* is wished away not only to the country of the Gandhāris but also further beyond, to that of the Bāhlikas. In the Brāhmaṇa literature we again come across with these people (*Śat. Br.* 1,7,3-5). Two new people are also spoken of—the Uttarakurus and the Uttaramadras as distinguished from the Kurus and the Madras settled in the Punjab (*Ait. Br.* VIII, 14, 23). The next writer Yāska who comes immediately after, speaks of another new people—the Kāmbojas probably for the first time (*Nirukta*, II, 2).

The Bāhlikas are well known. It appears that the Uttarakurus, Uttaramadras as well as the Kāmbojas too belonged to the still undefined region of Central Asia beyond the Himalayas. The existence of an Uttarakuru in this region is noted by the Greek writers till the fifth century A. D. Ptolemy is the first to speak of a town named Ottorokorrha and of a river and a mountain bearing the same name in the Serique (Chinese Turkestan) near the mountain Emodos (Himalaya). Later writers speak of the same place under the name Oporrocorra (*apara* and *uttara* here having the same meaning), The tradition survived till the 5th century as Orosius still speaks of the Ottorogorras. The name Uttaramadra might suggest a connection with the Median tribes (the Madā) and an attempt was made a few years ago to prove that the Maddas or the Madras of the Punjab were Median immigrants to India. Amongst the reasons adduced in favour of this hypothesis stress has been laid on the unorthodox customs prevalent amongst them and mentioned by the *Mahābhārata.* The epic distinctly speaks of the king of the Madras as Bāhlika-puṅgava and thus suggests his connection with the Iranian world.

The Kāmbojas also point out to the same direction. Although they are constantly associated with Gandhāra still it is impossible to find out their trace on the frontiers of India. The name of Gandhāra survived for long centuries but that of the Kāmbojas were soon forgotten. This makes it probable that they belonged to the nomad hordes of Central Asia which were moving from place to place. One of their branches seem to have entered India in very early times but they must have soon lost their identity as a distinct people. Other branches of the same people seem to have entered Eastern Tibet and the valley of the Mekong from another direction. By this assumption only we can explain why the name Kambuja was given to the kingdom founded in the middle valley of the Mekong. In Eastern Tibet also their name can be traced in the name of the province of Khams and it is probably from this region that the Kāmboja invasion of Assam and Bengal took place in later times.

In the early Buddhist texts, the Epics as well as the Purāṇas we get a more elaborate scheme to systematise the geographical knowledge possessed by the Indians not only of India but also of other Asiatic regions. The principles which guided the compilers of these texts are not always evident but as some of their notions correspond to actuality it is not fair to reject the cosmology presented by them as fanciful.

The Buddhist texts mention four continents spread around the central mount Meru in the following order : in the South Jambudvīpa, in the North Uttara-Kuru, in the West Apara-Godāna and in the East Pūrva-Videha. Jambudvīpa was generally speaking India, according to the Buddhists. Uttara-Kuru, as we have seen, was the name given to Chinese Turkestan. Godāna was the name by which Khotan was known in ancient times. The oldest form of the name of Khotan is preserved in the Chinese transcription of the Han period as Yu-t'ien. The Chinese words were pronounced in the Han period as *(*g*) *iu-den* i. e. Godāna. The name Apara-Godāna thus seems to have been used with reference to the region of Khotan. Pūrva-Videha must have meant the eastern zone to the east of Videha— Videha being the eastern limit of the North Indian world at the time when this geographical notion was first formed.

The Brahmanical cosmology which is sensibly of a later period gives us a more elaborate scheme. Jambudvīpa according to it is no longer India alone but the entire central belt of the continent as known to the compilers of that age. It is divided into seven *varṣas* or regions of which the first is the Bhāratavarṣa or India. Another known varṣa is Uttara-Kuru. The five other varṣas are Kiṁpuruṣa, Hari, Bhadrāśva, Ketumāla, Ilāvṛta and Ramayaka. As the central mountain of Kiṁpuruṣavarṣa is mentioned as Hemakūṭa it is possible that this was the name given to the Himalayan zone Ilāvṛta might suggest a connection with the region watered by the Ili river further to the north. Jambudvīpa is again only one of the seven continents. Amongst the other continents two, the Śāka dvīpa and the Krauñcadvīpa, have been described in detail in the *Mahābhārata*. As we shall see later on, at least the former corresponded to reality.

But although we cannot do full justice to the cosmological notions contained in the Buddhist and Brahmanical texts, there is ample evidence to show that the Indian compilers were acquainted with most of the people of the Central Asiatic regions in the age when these cosmological notions were systematised. For example one of the early Sanskrit Buddhist texts mentions—Cīna Kauśika, Khaśa, Bāhlī, Tukhāra, Pahlava, Pārata, Śaka, Vokkaṇa Ramaṭha. The *Rāmāyaṇa* locates to the North of Gāndhāra and Madraka—the Yavana, Śaka, Pārada, Bāhlika, Ṛṣika, Paurava, Kiṁkara, Cīna, Apara-Cīna, Tukhāra, Barbara, Kāmboja, Darada, Kirāta, Taṅkana, Paśupāla. The *Mahābhārata* speaks of the

Yavana, Cīna, Kāmboja, Sakṛdgraha, Kulattha, Hūṇa, Pāraśika Ramaṇa (*sic.* Ramaṭha), Ābhira, Darada, Kāśmīra, Paśu(pāla), Khasira (? Khasa), Pañhava (Pahlava), Girigahvara etc. amongst the people living in the North. The Purāṇas locate in the same region : Bāhlika, Vāṭadhāna, Ābhira, Kālatoyaka, Pallava, Carmakhaṇḍika, Pārada, Hārabhuṣika, Daśamālika, Kāmboja, Darada, Barbara, Harṣavardhana, Cīna, Tukhāra, Culika, Śūlika etc. The *Bṛhatsaṃhitā* attempts at a more precise classification : in the West—Haihaya, Vokkaṇa, Ramaṭha, Pārata, Śaka ; in the NW—Tuṣāra, Madra, Kulūta, Carmaraṅga, Ekavilocana (Ekanetra), Śūlika ; in the N—Kuru, Uttara-Kuru, Vāṭadhāna, Huṇa and in the NE—Paśupāla, Cīna, Khaśa, Ghoṣa, Kucika.

I will not waste your valuable time on the identification of these tribes, many of which are known to us from previous researches. Yavana, Śaka, Pārada, Kāmboja, Hūṇa, Pāraśika, Cīna are well-known. The Tuṣāras or Tukhāras were the people of Tokharestan. The Carmakhaṇḍikas are supposed to have been the people of Samarcand. The Śūlikas, also known as Cūlikas were the Sogdians. The Kucikas or Kuśikas may be identified with the ancient people of Kucī or Kucha. Vokkaṇa is identified with Wakhan. The Ekavilocanas remind us of the one-eyed people whom Herodotus locates in the extreme North of Central Asia above the Issedones. The Taṅganas or Taṇkanas may have been connected with the Doṅki or the Tunguse. Although we cannot identify other tribes in the lists referred to above the identities already noted are quite sufficient to prove that from about the second century B. C. to about 500 A. D. the Indian writers possessed a fairly accurate knowledge of the nomadic hordes that were moving about in Central Asia. The cosmological notions recorded by these writers reveal that they possessed also a fairly precise knowledge of the lands beyond the Himalayas. Compared with this, the Greek sources, although indispensable for our modern studies, do not appear to be of any greater value.

Under these circumstances I should like to attach a greater importance than hitherto done to the Puranic accounts of the foreign dynasties that ruled in India after the fall of the Imperial Andhras. The accounts say :

"When the kingdom of the Andhras has come to an end there will be kings belonging to the lineage of their servants: 7 Andhras, and 10 Ābhīra kings, also 7 Gardabhins, 18 Śakas. There will be 8 Yavanas, 14 Tuṣāras, 13 Muruṇḍas and 11 Hūṇas (or Maunas)."

"The Śrīparvatīya Andhras will endure 52 years, the Ābhīra kings 67 years, Gardabhins 72 years, the 18 Śakas 183 years, the 8 Yavanas 87 years, The earth is remembered as belonging to the Tuṣāras 7000 years, according to some accounts 500 (but apparently either 107 or 105 is meant). The 13 future Muruṇḍas along with low caste men, all of mleccha origin will enjoy it half 400 years (i. e. 200 years). The 11 Maunas will enjoy it 103 years. When they are overthrown by time there will be Kailakila kings. Then after the Kilakilas, Vindhyaśakti will reign. He will enter upon the earth after it has known those kings 96 years."

The Ābhīras and Gardabhins mentioned in the list are regarded as kings of foreign origin but we know almost nothing about them. The Yavanas or the Bactrian Greeks have been recently treated by M. Tarn, a recognised authority in classical studies. I propose to discuss here the problems concering the Śaka, the Tuṣāra, the Muruṇḍa and the Hūṇa.

THE SAKA PROBLEM

If we take the Puranic accounts literally we have to admit that the Śaka conquerors preceded the Yavanas or the Greeks in India. At least they were elder contemporaries in their Indian adventures. The Puranic evidence has however not been given any credence for want of corroborative facts. The Chinese evidence has been relied upon to prove that the Śakas could not have entered India before the commencement of the 1st century B. C. The Greek rule had been established in the Punjab and in the Kabul valley about a century earlier. In fact this is regarded as the reason for which the Śakas came to India not directly by the Kabul route but from Drangiana which they had conquered in the middle of second century. Let us now examine the evidences again and see how far they are precise enough to admit of such interpretation.

The Greek writers from the time of Herodotus speak of the Śakas as a branch of the Scythic people which occupied Central Asia in early times. Herodotus says that the Persians used the designation Śaka in a loose way. Strabo (58 B. C.- 21A. D.) tells us that the Caucasus separated the Sakai, the Scythes and the Seres in the North from the Indians in the South. Ptolemy in the second century A. D. says that the eastern frontier of the Sakai was Scythia.

The Old Persian Inscriptions speak more clearly of the Śakas than the Greek texts. Thus in the Behistun Inscription there is mention of Bactria, Sogdiana, Gandhāra, Śaka, Tathagush, Arachosia and Maka, and again after Parthia of Margiana, Tathagush and Śaka provinces which revolted against Darius. In the Persepolis inscription we are told that the eastern provinces of the empire were Arachosia, India, Gandhāra, Śaka and Maka. In the Nakshi Rustum Inscription there is mention of Zranka (Drangiana), Arachosia, Tathagush, Gandhāra, India, Śaka Haumavarka, Śaka Tigrakhauda, and in the Gold Tablet Inscription of Darius we are told that his empire extended from Śaka beyond Sogdiana (para-sugdam) to Ethiopia and from India to Sardis. The Śaka Tigrakhauda or the "Śakas who wore pointed helmets" were according to Herodotus the neighbours of the Bactrians and most probably occupied the Jaxartes region. The Śaka Haumavarka who were the same as the Amyrgian Scythians of Herodotus were those who had settled in the Persian Province of Drangiana. The Behistun and the Persepolis inscriptions really locate them near Gandhāra. The old Persian Inscriptions therefore make it clear that the Śakas were living near the frontiers of India long before the Greeks had come to that region.

The Indian literature speaks of them but only at a time when the Greeks had settled in Bactria. This is the reason for which the Śakas are closely associated with the Yavanas in these texts specially in the *Rāmāyaṇa*, the *Manusaṃhitā* and the *Mahābhārata*. But a particular chapter of the *Mahābhārata*, inserted in the Bhīṣmaparva which gives the description of the Śākadvīpa or "the land of the Śakas" seems to bear an earlier stamp. It is said that there are seven mountains in Śākadvīpa, named Meru, Malaya, Jaladhara, Raivata, Śyāma, Durgaśaila and Keśara. The land is divided into seven varṣas : *Mahākāśa* near Meru, *Kumudottara* near Malaya, *Sukumāra* near Jaladhara, *Kaumāra* near Raivata, *Maṇikāñcana* near Śyāma, *Maudākī* near Keśara and *Mahāpuruṣa* near Durgaśaila. The text then says that there are four Janapadas or kingdoms in the land of the Śakas, *Maga* (or *Maṅga*), *Maśaka*, *Mānasa* and *Mandaga*. These regions are watered by different branches of the Ganges viz. Sukumāri Śītāśī, Venikā, Manijalā, Cakṣu (i. e. Vakṣu), and Vardhanikā. Regarding the character of the people the text then says that the Magas are Brahmin by vocation, Maśakas Kṣatriya, the Mānasas Vaiśya and the Mandagas Sūdra.

According to Rapson this Śākadvīpa would be the name given to the lower Indus valley after the Śakas had settled there in the first cencutry B. C. This identification has been suggested by the use of the word *dvīpa* in this connection. The word dvīpa however was used in the Puranic and Epic cosmology in a much broader sense and not in the narrow sense of island. Then again there is little doubt about the identification of the river Vakṣu (Oxus) which flowed through the country of the Śakas. Another river, the Śītāśī may be the same as the Sītā which is the name given to the Yarkand river in some texts. According to an old notion all the four rivers, Gaṅgā, Sindhu, Vakṣu and Sītā, issued from the same source, the Anavatapta lake and hence they could be known under the same name Ga gā. Of the four people mentioned above the Maga reminds us of the Magians, the Maka of the old Persian inscriptions who according to Herodotus were a Median tribe. The Maśakas may be very well identified with the Massagetae another Scythic people mentioned by Herodotus as a powerful and valiant people dwelling towards the east beyond the river Araxes over against the Issedonians. It may be noted that thy Maśakas are also described in the *Mahābhārata* as Kṣatriyas. The Mandagas or Madagas might have been the same as the Mada or the Medes. The names of two of the *varṣas* seem to correspond to things known from other sources. Kumudottara may be connected with the Komedoi of the Greek writers which extended from the Oxus to the river of Karategin. Mahākāśa reminds us of Akhasa which the classical authors place in Scythia. The difficulty in identifying the names of mountains and rivers is due to the fact that the old names have often been replaced by new ones in this region.

That the Śakas were known in India before the establishment of the Greek rule is also indirectly suggested by the Jaina account as preserved in the *Kālakācāryakathānaka.* In order to punish the autocratic Gardabhillas of Ujjayinī Kālaka sought for outside help. He could have gone to the Yavanas as well had they been settled in the upper Indus valley. But instead of doing that he went to the Sagakula i. e. the Śaka race beyond the Indus. He induced some of the Śaka chiefs to accompany him. They crossed the Indus in ships and went to Kathiawar. These chiefs first occupied the kindom of Surāṣṭra and divided the country amongst themselves. Next they went up Ujjayinī, imprisoned the Gardabhilla king and set up one of their chiefs as ruler there. In course of time (*kālāntareṇa*) Vikramāditya the king of Mālava ousted the Śaka dynasty and established his own era (58 B. C.). This dynasty also was destroyed by another Śaka ruler after 135 years of the Vikrama era had elapsed (78 A. D.). Prof. Sten Konow has given full credence to this story. The route followed by the Śaka chiefs indicates that they were coming from the other side of the Indus, probably from Seistan where Śaka settlements had been established already in the Achaemenian period. But how long did they rule in Ujjayinī before the rise of this legendary Vikramāditya in 58 B. C. is not known. The account vaguely says *kālāntareṇa* : after a lapse of time. Prof. Konow has referred to a late Jaina tradition which says that the Śakas ruled at Ujjayinī only for four years. Accordingly the Śaka occupation of Ujjayinī may be placed in 61-60 B. C. But the same account attributes a reign of only 13 years to the Gardabhillas. A little examination shows that it is only a distorted version of the Puranic accounts which however assign a reign of 183 years to the Śakas and 72 years to the Gardabhillas.

One of the oldest Śaka rulers of India, Maues had extended his rule up to Taxila and Gandhara but we do not know from which direction. Most of the scholars now agree that it was from the Śaka settlements in the lower Indus valley. But we should not forget that although some of his coins appear as imitations of the coins of Demetrios and Appollodotus the great majority of them bear Parthian influence in the regal formula—Basileus basileum Megaloy Mayoy. Orosius speaks of a Parthian invasion of India up to the Hydaspes by Mithradates I (171-138 B. C.). But this account has been given little credence for insufficient reasons.

If we attach less importance to the story of the foundation of a powerful Greek kingdom extending from the Kabul valley to the Punjab after the invasion of Demetrios, and Menander—a kingdom which would be a sort of impenetrable barrier against a possible Parthian or Śaka invasion from the side of Bactria then we can explain things more clearly. The Śakas had undergone a great Parthian influence, the language they spoke was the Eastern Iranian dialect and they had rendered a great help in the foundation of the Arsacidan dynasty. So a possible Parthian invasion of the Punjab by Mithradates I, as Orosius tells us, might have brought the Śakas to the Punjab along the Kabul valley. The Greek opposition would be futile in that case. The Śakas of Kathiawar and Ujjayini represented an altogether different branch of the same people that had penetrated through the lower Indus valley at a much earlier period possibly with local help as the *Kālakācāryakathanaka* would have us believe.

What is then the importance of the Chinese account regarding the movement of the Śaka people from the region of Ta-hia? The annals of the former Han dynasty *Ts'ien Han shu* contain the following account which is now well-known:

> "Formerly when the Hiung-nu subjugated the Ta Yue-che the latter migrated to the West and gained the dominion over Ta-hia whereupon the king of Sai moved south and ruled over Ki-pin. The Sai were scattered and at times formed several kingdoms. North-West of Shu-lei, the Hou-sun, Sun-tu and consanguinous nations are all descendants of the ancient Sai.'

The Chinese word Sai was pronounced in Han times *Sek* and hence it is certain that the word was used to render the name of the Śakas (Greek Saces). The Ta Yue-ches were defeated by the Hiung-nus in 176 B. C. They ousted the Śakas from the Jaxartes region in about 160 B. C. The Śakas then migrated to Ta-hia (later Tokharestan). Pressed by the Wu-suns the Yue-ches moved to the south and occupied Ta-hia. It was then that the King of the Śakas was obliged to move further south and to go to Ki-pin. This must have taken place before 128 B. C.

The route to Ki-pin which the Śaka king followed is clearly stated. He passed the *Hien-tu* or the hanging passage while moving towards Ki-pin from his original seat in Ta-hia. This route was recognised by Chavannes and Sir Aurel Stein as the Bolor route through the Yasin valley. This was the route which was usually followed by the ancient travellers from the region of Wakhan to the Indus valley and to Kashmir and Udyāna.

If we follow this Chinese account literally we are driven to two conclusions ; the first, that the Śakas who were turned out of Ta-hia by the Yue-ches entered India by the Bolor route and the second, that Ki-pin which they conquered was Kashmir. The first conclusion has been discarded on the ground that the Bolor route was impracticable and the second has been rejected on the ground that Ki-pin could not be Kashmir but must be identified with Kabul-Kapiśa. It has therefore been supposed that the Śakas went south from Ta-hia and as it was impossible for them to enter the Kabul valley owing to the presence of the Greeks in that region they went westwards to the direction of Herat and thence southwards to Seistan. From Seistan they entered India by the lower valley of the Indus in the first century B. C. and thence extended their influence northwards to the Kabul valley.

I think that this assumption is not necessary at all. The Śakas of Ta-hia seem to have represented an entirely different group and had no relation with the Śakas of Seistan. The Bolor route again was not probably so impracticable as has been supposed. At least it does not appear to have been impracticable in the end of the 4th century A. D. when the first Chinese traveller, Fa-hien and his associates came to India.

Then again the identification of Ki-pin with Kabul-Kapiśā is an impossibility. Lévi and Chavannes were the first to propose the identification of Ki-pin of the Chinese annals with Kashmir. They pointed out that in a number of Chinese translations of Buddhist texts the translators use Ki-pin for translating the name Kashmir up to 581 A. D. Since 581 A. D. the Bundhist translations as well as other Chinese documents use the name Ki-pin to denote Kapiśā and not Kashmir. In recent years there has been a tendency to take these conclusions too lightly. For example Tarn in his book "The Greeks in Bactria and India" while identifying Ki-pin with Kophene (Kabul) refers to Lévi only to point out that "the Chinese mixed up Kapiśā and Kashmir in their Ki-pin." The Chinese writers made this confusion only after 581 A. D. as Ki-pin had by then become too old a name to convey a precise geographical import. But there is no ground to believe that the same confusion existed prior to 581 A. D. In the oldest Chinese translation of the Milindapañha which belong to the 4th century A. D. Káśmīra of the original text is twice rendered in Chinese as Ki-pin. The Chinese biography of Kumārajīva contains another corroborative evidence. Kumārajīva was taken from Kucha to Kashmir by his mother for proper education in the third quarter of the 4th century A. D. Kashmir was then a reputed centre of Sanskrit learning. While coming from the west they crossed the river Sin-t'ou (Sindhu) in order to go to Kashmir which is called Ki-pin. Of the description of Ki-pin which we get in the Chinese annals of the Han and Wei periods, the following points may be noted : (i) Ki-pin was to the South-East of Ta Yue-che i. e. Ta-hia. The kingdom of Nan-tu was at 9 days journey to its North-East and Wu-yi-shan-li to the South-West. Nan-tu seems to be *Dar-du i. e. Darada. Wu-yi-shan-li which is a transcription of the name Alexandria has been identified with Kandahar. (ii) The valley of Ki-pin was surrounded by hill ranges on four sides. It was a flat country having a length of 800 li from East to West and a breadth of 300 li from the North to the south. These accounts seem to refer clearly to Kashmir and not to

Kabul-Kapiśā. The name Ki-pin itself seems to suggest the same. In Han pronounciation the first word *Ki* was definitely a **Ka* probably followed by some consonant which might have been a *s*. Pin was pronounced almost certainly in early time *pir* or *wir*. Hence Ki-pin clearly stood for **Ka*(s)-*pir* or **Ka*(s)-*wir*. This form of the name is also found in the early Greek records in which Kashmir is either Caspiri or Kaspeira. Ki-pin was thus a correct phonetic transcription of the old name of Kashmir. The Śakas of Ta-hia could not have come to Kashmir via Seistan and the lower Indus valley— they must have come there by the shorter route—i. e. the Bolor route from Ta-hia.

THE TUKHARA PROBLEM

The next problem is what I should like to call the Tukhāra or Tokharian problem. In the dynastic lists of the Purāṇas it is said that the Tuṣāra kings succeeded the Yavanas in India. Their number is given as 14. According to the *Matsya* the world belonged to them for seven thousand years (*sapta-varṣa-sahasrāṇi*) whereas according to the *Vāyu* and *Brahmāṇḍa* they ruled for *pañca-varṣa-śatāni* which may be interpreted either as five hundred years or as 105 years. Five hundred years would be too long a period for 14 kings and so it is just probable that they ruled only for 105 years. The *Matsya* account may be accordingly corrected as *sapta-varṣa-śatān-iha* and interpreted as 107 years. Some of the early Purāṇas give Tukhāra as a variant of Tuṣāra. It is certain that the cerebral was pronounced as *kha* when the name was adopted by the Puranic chroniclers. The *Rāmāyaṇa* gives the name as Tukhāra. The name is given in the same form by the *Mahābhārata* as well as by two old Buddhist texts the *Saddharma -smṛtyupasthāna* and the *Mahāmayūrī*. The Chinese pilgrims tell us that the Tukhāra Buddhists like the Ceylonese had a special monastery built for them at the Mahabodhi in the 7th century. In the same century Bāṇa writes in his *Harṣacarita* that Harṣa used to get taxes from the mountainous and inaccessible region of the Tuṣāras (*atra parameśvareṇa tuṣāraśailabhuvo durgāyāḥ gṛhītaḥ karaḥ*) This only shows that Tukhāra as a distinct people and the land of the Tukhāras (Tokharestan) as a distint country in the mountainous regions beyond the frontiers of India were known to the Indians as late as the middle of the 7th century A. D.

The classical authors mention the people under the same name. Thus Pliny says—"After the Attacores (the same as Ottorokorras) come the Phuni (Phruni), Thocari and Casiri (which seems to be a mistake for Caspiri), the last belonging to India." Ptolemy speaks of them as Thagouroi, Periegetes (2nd century) and all later writers up to the 4th century as Tochari. The Tokharians therefore according to these sources were a central Asian people living to the North of the Caspiri or Kashmir.

The Chinese sources of the Han period speak of a people named Ta-hia. They were living as early as the 2nd century B. C. in the Oxus region. The two Chinese words *Ta* and *hia* were pronounced in early times as D'a(t)-g'a and it stood in all probability for the name Dogār or Tukhār. From the 5th century the name appears in the Chinese annals as T'u-ho-lo *T'u-χuo-la i. e. Tukhāra. The king of that country sent ambassadors to China in 453, 457 and 465 A. D. At the time when Hiuan-tsang visited the country it had passed into the hands of the Western Turks. The pilgrim tells us that Tokharestan in that period was a very extensive kingdom. It reached the Tsong-ling (the Pamirs) on the East, Persia on the West, the Hindukush on the South and the Iron Pass or Derbend in the North. The Oxus flowed through this country. Henceforth contact with China remained almost uninterrupted for about two centuries. It is in this period that the Tibetan texts speak of the country of Tho-gar or Tho-dgar and of the Buddhists monks of that country who had gone to Tibet to participate in the work of translation of Buddhist texts. The Uigurs also speak of them as Toxri and of their country as Twxrstn i. e. Tokharestan.

We therefore see that from about the second century B. C. to about the middle of the 7th century A. D. all sources of information, Sanskrit, Greek, Latin and Chinese concur in recognising a people called Tukhāra living in the country which came to be known in later times as Tokharestan. The original seat of the people was the Upper valley of the Oxus in the region of Badakshan. The Puranic sources would have us believe that kings of this Tukhāra origin conquered India from the Greeks and set up their own rule. Fourteen of their rulers reigned in India for a little over one hundred years.

These are precisely the rulers who are designated Kushan by the modern historians of India. The Greek legends on the coins of these rulers give them the name Korsano Kosano, etc. and the Kharoṣṭhī Inscriptions Kuṣana, Khuṣana and Kuṣana. The name of a king of this group of rulers called Mahārāja Guṣana may be connected with the same name. The occurrence of the initial letter as *g*, *k*, *kh*, and Greek *k* and *x* shows that it was probably a guttural fricative which could not be exactly rendered into an Indian form. Prof. Konow probably rightly considers that the word is an Iranian form with the genitive plural suffix of *āna* which is used as a rule with the Iranian ethnic names. In that case the base would be Guṣa or Kuṣa. In fact one of the Kushan rulers, Kanishka is described as a member of the Kuśa race in a Buddhist text ascribed to Aśvaghoṣa who according to the Buddhist tradition was contemporaneous with that great ruler.

In order to explain the origin of this family name an evidence contained in the old Han annals has been referred to. According to it the Kuṣaṇas would be the same as Kui-shuanga branch of the Ta Yue-che nomads. The passage which contains this evidence occurs in the annals of the later Han dynasty *Hou Han shu*. Let us consider this passage again :

"Previously the Yue-ches were conquered by the Hiung-nus. They then went away to Ta-hia and divided this kingdom into five hi-hou namely Hiu-mi, Shuang-mi, Kui-shuang, Hi-tun and Tu-mi. More than one hundred years after this the hi-hou of Kui-shuang named K'iu-tsiu-k'io attacked and vanquished the four other hi-hou, called himself king and the name of his kingdom become Kui-shuang. He invaded Ngan-si, conquered Kao-fu, became victorious over P'u-ta and Ki-pin and possessed these kingdoms entirely. K'iu-tsiu-k'io died at the age of more than 80 years. His son Yen-kao-chen became

17

king in his place ; in his turn he conquered T'ien-chu (India) and established there a chief to administer it. From this time the Yue-ches became extremely powerful. All the different countries call their king, the king of Kui-shuang but the Han call them Ta Yue-che retaining their ancient title."

The names of the two kings K'iu-tsiu-k'io and Yen-kao-chen have been corrected as K'iu-tsio-kie and Yen-kao-mi by no less a Chinese authority than Prof. Pelliot. When these corrections are admitted the names appear in their archaic pronunciation as K'ieu-dz'ieu-kiāp and Iam-kau-mjie. These may be restored accurately as Kuju Kapa and Vema Kaβi which are exactly the names of Kujula Kadaphises and Wema Kadaphises. According to the latest interpretation of the passage it would appear that the five hi-hou belonged to the old kingdom of Ta-hia i. e. the Tukhāra. They temporarily became vassals of the Ta Yue-che but later on the hi-hou of Kui-shuang supplanted the Yue-che rule and established his own. He was therefore a Tukhāra but the Chinese writers followed the old custom and continued to call them Ta Yue-che. Thus Kujulo Kadphises who supplanted the Yue-che rule was primarily a Tukhāra and secondarily a Kui-shuang. So far as the first appellation is concerned the Indian sources amply confirm it. It was the Tukhāras who followed the Greeks in India and they were not known by any other name. As Chinese evidence shows, Kui-shuang was the name of the principality over which Kujula ruled as a hi-hou. This was the name given to the kingdom founded by him after the overthrow of the Yue-che rule simply because the nucleus of that kingdom was his own principality. Kui-shuang was not an ethnic name and hence the Sanskrit sources do not mention it but retain the name Tukhāra.

The connection between Kui-shuang and Kuṣaṇa is not very clear. Kuei-shuang, in old pronunciation Kjwei-siang, was something like Khuṣaṇa or Kuṣaṇa. Kadphises I uses both Koṣano and Xosano on his coins. In the Panjtar inscription of the year 122 there is mention of a Mahārāja Guṣana and in the Taxila silver scroll Inscription of the year 136 there is mention of Mahārāja Rājātirāja Devaputra Khuṣaṇa. The titles show that they were two different rulers but who they were, we do not know. There is again reference to the Guṣaṇavaṃśa and its scion General Lala in the year 18 of Kaniṣka in the Manikiala Stone Inscription.

This uncertainty in the use of the name Kuṣaṇa is more the reason why we should attach greater importance to the ethnic name Tukhāra given not only in the Purāṇas but also in all other sources.

We have said that the Tukharas were not the Ta Yue-ches. They continued to be so called by the Chinese historians by mistake. The Ta Yue-ches had probably merged into the Tukhāra people and adopted the local culture. This is the reason why they are only vaguely remembered by the Chinese historians. They are last mentioned only in connection with the Kidarites. A Chinese annal (Pei-she) tell us that king Ki-to-lo (Kidāra) of Ta Yue-che, driven by the Juan-juan shifted to the town of Po-lo (B'ak-la : Balkh) and then conquered Northern India and the 4 kingdoms to the North of Gāndhāra. The annal then says that Kidāra had asked his son to occupy the city of Fu-lu-sha (Puruṣapura) and that this is the reason why the kingdom of his son was called Siao Yue-che or Little Yue-che.

This brings us to another question, that of the Little Yue-ches. Some scholars are still inclined to hold that Kaniṣka belonged to the Little Yue-che and that he entered India from Chinese Turkestan by a different route. The late Baron de Stael Holstein was the first to put forward this theory. He was of opinion that the Kidarites were called Little Yue-che because the tradition of the Little Yue-che was being perpetuated at Peshawar by the successors of Kaniṣka. But we have seen that the Chinese text is quite clear on this point. The text first speaks of the Great Yue-che kingdom of Kidāra and then of the kingdom founded at Peshawar by his son. The latter was called Little Yue-che so that it could be distinguished from the kingdom of the father. The annalist had no knowledge of the fact that there was a king called Kaniṣka and that his capital was at Peshawar. And he was writing in the middle of the 5th century A. D.

There is a slight earlier evidence on the Little Yue-ches. In a

Buddhist text translated in 413 Kumārajīva translates the name Tukhāra as Siao Yue-che or Little Yue-che. Kumārajīva was a native of Central Asia and therefore the information supplied by him on this point should be seriously considered. Prof. Pelliot would like to explain it thus: "After the rupture of relation between China and the West in the last quarter of the 3rd century the Great Yue-ches had been forgotten in China. Only the Little Yue-ches were spoken of. As Kumārajīva was writing for the Chinese he used the terminology known to them in his times and rendered the name Tukhāra as Little Yue-che because they were the only Yue-ches whose name was still understood. Otherwise it is inconceivable that a native of Central Asia would explain the name Tukhāra as Little Yue-che who had never come to Ta-hia and had been driven by the Hiung-nus to the South-East to Kan-su".

There is therefore no reason to think that Kaniṣka was a Little Yue-che. The Little Yue-ches had lost their identity amongst the barbarians of South-Eastern China just as the Great Yue-ches had lost theirs amongst the Tukhāras. Besides these Little Yue-ches had no connection either with Ta-hia (Tukhāra) or with Kui-shuang (Kuṣaṇa).

There is another point to which I should like to draw your attention in this connection. It is the confusion in late literature between two different names, the Tukhāra and the Turuṣka. In the *Garuḍa* and *Vāmana Purāṇas* we have Turuṣka and Turaṣka in the place where we should have expected Tukhāra or Tuṣāra. Kalhaṇa while speaking of the Shahi rulers of Afganistan who claimed descent from Kaniṣka calls them Turuṣka. Hemacandra in his *Abhidhānacintāmaṇi* probably refers to the same Shahi rulers as Turuṣka sākhi (959-Turuṣkāstu sākha yaḥ syuḥ). But we know definitely that the Turuṣkas were the Turks and different from the Tukhāras. In a Chinese-Sanskrit lexicon of the 7th century A. D. which I edited a few years ago the Sanskrit name of the Tu-kius (Turks) is given as Truṣkagaṇa. Tokharestan had passed into the hands of the Western Turks in the 7th century and since then it was natural for all late Sanskrit writers to make an easy confusion between Tukhāra and Turuṣka just as the earlier

Chinese writers had done in calling the Tukhāras Yue-che after the Yue-che conquest of the country.

THE MURUNDA PROBLEM

Although the Muruṇḍas are regarded as a separate dynasty of rulers who succeeded the Tukhāras some scholars would consider them as identical with the Śakas. Prof. Sten Konow explains the word as a Śaka word meaning "Lord", "Master" and takes it to be identical with the Chinese expression Sai-wang "the king of the Śakas" which the annalists use in connection with the Śaka migration from Central Asia. Prof. Konow's reading and interpretation of the word muroḍa in the Zeda inscription is far from certain. Its connection with Muruṇḍa is still less probable.

On the contrary the Purāṇas consider the Muruṇḍas as quite distinct from the Śakas. All of them agree in stating that the Muruṇḍas followed the Tukhāras in India and that 13 of their kings ruled in India along with low caste men, all of Mleccha origin. The duration of their rule was according to some sources 400 years whereas according to other sources 200 years. Who were these Muruṇḍas ?

We know that the Muruṇḍas were in India before the foundation of the Gupta empire. The Allahabad Pillar Inscription of Samudragupta tells us that the Muruṇḍas were amongst those who accepted the vassalage of the Guptas. The name next occurs in the Khoh copperplate Inscription of the beginning of the sixth century. We are told there that the mother of the Mahārāja Sarvanātha of Ucchakalpa was Muruṇḍadevī, also called Muruṇḍasvāminī. She was so called probably because she was a princess of the Muruṇḍa dynasty.

The mention of the Muruṇḍas is found in earlier texts too. Prof. Lévi was the first to deal with these texts. The Chinese annals have preserved the record of a political mission which was sent to India from the Hinduised kingdom of Fu-nan in Indo-China in the 3rd century A. D. We are told that in the period 222-277 A. D. the king of Fu-nan sent one of his relatives to India. The ambassador started from Fu-nan, went out of the mouth of the river Tu-kiu-li (Takkola ?) and following the great bend of the littoral right towards the North-West entered a big gulf which bordered on different kingdoms. At the end of a little more than a year he entered the mouth of the river of T'ien-chu (India). He went up this river, covered a distance of about 700 li and arrived at his destination. The king of India was taken by surprise to learn that there were such men on the distant shores of the ocean. He sent with him various presents to the king of Fu-nan and amongst them there were four horses of the Yue-che country. The Indian ambassadors who went to Fu-nan along with this mission were met by the Chinese ambassador at the Funanese court. Being questioned he told the latter that the title of the king of India was *Mou-lun* and that the capital where he resided was guarded by two consecutive circles of ramparts and that the ditches were constantly fed by the water carried by cannals from the river. The description of the city and the palace as given by the Indian ambassadors reminds one of the splendour of Pāṭalīputra.

The Chinese name, as Prof. Lévi has shown, is a faithful transcription of the name Muruṇḍa. Ptolemy locates the Marundai in the same region, in Eastern India, on the right bank of the Ganges. The Jaina version of the *Siṁhāsana-dvātriṁśikā* tells us that a Muruṇḍa-rāja was the king of Kānyakubja. The *Prabandha-cintāmaṇi* of Merutuṅga tells us that the Muruṇḍarāja had his capital at Pāṭalīputra. Another Jaina legend would have us believe that Pādaliptasūri who was a contemporary of Nāgārjuna had cured a Muruṇḍarāja from a serious disease and coverted him to Jainism.

Although these evidences are few and insufficient they are conclusive enough to prove the existence of Muruṇḍa kings in India from the Kushan period up to the Gupta period. The geography of Ptolemy and the Chinese evidence discussed above difinitely show that the Muruṇḍas were established in Eastern India in the 2nd and 3rd centuries A. D. and that they possessed at least two important cities, Kānyakubja and Pāṭalīputra, the latter being probably their capital till the rise of the Guptas.

It is therefore permissible to suggest that the Muruṇḍas had come to India along with Tukhāras and that they had set up a kingdom in Eastern India first as vassals of the Tukhāras and then on their downfall as independent rulers. Their connection with the Yue-ches is suggested by the present of the four horses of the Yue-che country which they sent to Fu-nan. Then again when Hemacandra in his *Abhidhānacintāmaṇi* connects them with Lampāka (Lamghan) it does not mean that they were known in his times. He got this information from some older sources which knew that the Muruṇḍas had come by way of Lamghan. That was not the way followed by the Śakas in course of their invasion of India. The Śakas again had gone up to Western India and none of the old sources connect the Śakas with Pāṭalīputra. The Muruṇḍas therefore in all probability were a Tukhāra tribe like the Kushans and partially filled up the gap in the political history of India from the downfall of the Imperial Kushans to the rise of the Guptas. This fact was known to the Puranic chroniclers.

It seems we can trace the Muruṇḍas in Central Asia alongside the Tukhāras. The classical writers such as Strabo, Pliny and Periegetes speak of a people called Phrynoi who lived near the Tochari. If we are to believe the evidence of Pliny the Phrynoi or Phruni lived to the South of the mountain Attacoris, the Tochari lived to the south of the Phrynoi and the Casiri i. e. Caspiri or Kashmir to the South of the Tochari. The name of the Phrynoi could be very well rendered in Sanskrit as Mruṇḍa or Muruṇḍa. The Puranic chroniclers had probably some hesitation in rendering the name as such. Thus the *Vāyu-purāṇa* which is in many respects one of the most trustworthy texts render the name not exactly as Muruṇḍa or Muraṇḍa but as Puruṇḍa or Puraṇḍa. The cerebralisation of the original dental does not really make any difficulty as it has other examples too.

THE HUNA PROBLEM

The Hūṇa question, I believe, still remains a problem in Indian history. The reason is this. Kālidāsa in his *Raghuvaṃśa* in connection with the digvijaya of Raghu speaks of the Hūṇas as living on the banks of the Vakṣu or the Oxus. Prof. K. C. Chattopadhyaya in a very learned monograph on Kālidāsa has tried to establish the priority of Kālidasa on Aśvaghoṣa in the field of artificial poetry. He is of opinion that Kālidāsa lived in the first century B. C. If we accept this theory we have to admit that the Hūṇas were known in India already before the Christian era On the contrary we have so long maintained that the Hūṇas were not known in India before the fifth century. They appeared for the first time on the Indian soil in the time of Skandagupta (455-467 A. D.) under the distinctive name Hūṇa. They were at that time driven away. They appeared again towards the end of the same century and this time succeeded in establishing an independent Hūṇa kingdom in the Punjab. They ruled upto the second quarter of the sixth century as paramount rulers when they received a crushing defeat in the hands of Yaśodharman of Malwa.

These Hūṇas who appeared in India in fifth century A. D. were the Hepthalite Huns or the White Huns. Hepthal, Chinese Ye-t'a, was the eponymous hero of the race who in 484 A. D. defeated and killed Peroz, the king of Persia. In Iran the principal centres of these Huns were Badakshan and Bamiyan. It was in this region that Song-yun met them in the beginning of the sixth century. It was from this region that they penetrated into India. It has been so long maintained that they were the only Huns known in India.

But what about the old Hiung-nus of the Chinese annals ? After they had driven the Yue-ches away from the eastern part of Chinese Turkestan in the second century B. C. they continued to play an important political role in the history of Central Asia for long centuries. Such a powerful people must have been known to the Greek, Latin and Sanskrit writers long before the appearance of the Hepthalites. But under what name were they known ?

The Indian literature is not silent on the Hūṇas. The *Mahābhārata* speaks of the Hūṇas and generally in association with the Pāraśikas (*hunāḥ pāraśikaiḥ saha*). Amongst the Purāṇas the *Brahmāṇda* and the *Viṣṇu* only mention them. But none of these texts can be definitely placed before the 5th century A. D. The *Rāmāyaṇa* which bears the stamp of a more definite age does not mention the Hūṇas. The oldest translation of the *Mahāmāyūrī* which belongs to the 5th century does not either speak of the Hūṇas. Both these sources however know the Śakas, Yavanas and Palhavas.

The classical writers do not speak of the Hunnus before the sixth century. The earlier writers mention another people which may be identified with them. Thus Orosius who wrote in the beginning of the fifth century or towards the end of the 4th says : "Between the sources of the Ganges and those of the river Ottorogorras, situated to the North in the region of the Paropanisades mountains, the Taurus mountain extends. The Caucasus mountain extends between the sources of the Ottorogorras and the town of Ottorogorras through the country of the Chuni, Scythes and Gandarides." The variants given in the different manuscripts for Chuni are Chunos, Funos, Hunnus.

The Hiung-nu of the Chinese annals looks like the Hunnus of the Latin writers of the sixth century and like the Hūṇa of the Sanskrit literature and inscriptions mentioned, from the end of the fifth century onwards. We should however bear in mind that Hiung-nu is the pronunciation of about the same period. The earlier pronunciation of the Chinese name was Xiwong-nuo. It commenced with a guttural fricative which disappeared in later pronunciation. This guttural fricative was transcribed by the earlier classical writers as *Khu*. Towards the end of the fifth and the beginning of the sixth it had already changed into *Hu*. It is to this stage that the Latin Hunnus and Sanskrit Hūṇa belong.

It is thus clear that although the Hiung-nu hordes might have been known in India under a different name they could not be mentioned as Hūṇa before the fifth and sixth centuries A. D. In this connection I would propose to make another correction of a common error. A Roman historian of the 4th century tells us that in *circa* 358-360 A. D. the king of the Chionitae named Grumbates helped king Shapur II of Persia against the Romans in the siege of Amida. Cunningham suggested that the Chionitae were either the Kushans or the Tokharoi. But we have just seen that they were probably the same as Chuni or the Hiung-nus. It is possible that they were in this period quite mixed up with the Tokharoi but they cannot be on any account called Kushan.

The Puranic accounts tell us that the Muruṇḍa kings were followed in India by the Hūṇa rulers. Although some texts give the variant Mauna, Hūṇa seems to be the correct reading. They had eleven rulers who reigned for three hundred years. From the Inscriptions however we know only of two Hūṇa rulers namely Toramāṇa and Mihirakula. They reigned from about 490 A. D. to 540 A. D. Yaśodharaman's victory only put an end to the growth of the Hūṇas as an imperial power in India. The Hūṇa rule must have continued in the Punjab for several centuries that followed and the Puranic chroniclers are probably right in attributing to them a reign of about 300 years. It was the disintegration of the Hūṇa kingdom in the Punjab that led to the rise of different ruling clans in Northern India.

The problem of the Hūṇas is interconnected with the problem of the rise of some of the early medieval dynasties in Nothern India and although these problems fall outside the scope of our section I shall take the liberty of making some suggestions regarding them here. I will not enter into the origin of the Rajput clans who are now regarded by most of the scholars as of Scythic or Hūṇa origin. My remarks will be confined only to the consideration of certain facts which have not been so far properly noted. The first of this concerns the origin of the Gurjaras. They are looked upon as a Hūṇa race although their name has not been as yet traced to any Central Asian source. In order to do this we have probably to go to the old race movements in that region. The Han annals speak of three different people the Hiung-nu, the Wu-sun and the Yue-che. When the Hiung-nus turned out the Yue-ches from their original home the latter were compelled to migrate first to the country of the Wu-sun which was in the region of the Ili river. The Wu-sun subsequently drove the Yue-ches out of their country with the help of the Hiung-nus. We are told in this connection that the minor king of the Wu-sun was brought up amongst the Hiung-nus. It is just possible that the Wu-sun had Hun affinities. The old pronunciation of the name 'Uo-suen in all likelihood commenced with a consonant which was later on dropped and that consonant was most probably a guttural. In the 4th century the name was something like *Gusur* which gave rise to the name Gujar. The Wu-sun or the Gujars must have moved to India along with the Huns in the fifth century A. D. and on the downfall of the Hun kingdom set up their own rule.

The Turks were also of Hun origin. The ancestors of the Turks were a group of Hiung-nu families bearing the clan name Assena. The word Türk in old Turkish meant "mighty." The Chinese name Tu-kiu was based on a Mongol plural Türk-küt. The Sanskrit name Turuṣka was establised through such intermediate forms as Turuk, Turukkhu. The Turkish power rose in the 6th century and in the 7th century, shortly after 638 A. D., the chief of the Turks drove back the Persians to the West and conquered all the old Hepthalite dominions up to the frontiers of Kabul. The Turks had taken Balkh and Herat as early as the year 589 and in 599 we hear that they were assisting their vassals the Kushans and the Hepthalites against the Armenians and the Persians.

The Turks had a hierarchical organisation beginning with the princes of the blood up to the officer of high ranks. The first was called *teghin* who were princes of the blood. The officers of the highest official rank were called *Kuluchür*. It was suggested long ago that the Sanskrit word Ṭhākura was an adaptation of the Turkish word *teghin*. It is just possible that the dynastic name Kalachuri is also of Turkish origin. The founders of the dynasty were at first the Kuluchür or the highest Turkish officials. They had set up an independent kingdom when the central power had weakened. It is to be noted in this connection that the Kalachuris claimed descent from Sahasrabāhu Arjuna. In spite of the fact that the latter is celebrated in Indian mythology he reminds us of Assena from whom the innumerable Turkish hordes claimed their descent. If we thus assume that the Turks had come to India along with the Huns or shortly after them we can explain a significant reference to them in a Haihaya Inscription. We are told in this inscription that Kokkalla "plundered the treasuries of Karnāṭa, Vaṅga, Gurjara, Konkana and Śākambhari kings and also those born of the Turuṣka and Raghu families." The Gurjara-Pratihāras claimed descent from the Raghu family. But who were those born of the Turuṣkas? I believe that they were the Kalachuris and such other Turkish tribes as had followed the Huns in India.

* * *

I have now come to the end of my address. If I have not quite solved the problems, I hope I have succeeded in impressing on you that the problems exist. The migration of the Central Asian nomads to India is an essential corollary to the Indo-Iranian conquest which brought the Vedic civilisation to this country. The Central Asian nomads represented other ramifications of the same civilisation that spread from eastern Iran right up to the frontiers of China through mountain gorges and desert sands. Hence their contribution to the development of Indian civilisation increased its complexity by introducing traits that were analogous but distinct in forms. This phenomenon repeated itself almost in every age throughout the period with which we are just now concerned. I therefore believe that not only the political history but also the history of the art, society and religion of the entire period has to be studied against this wider background. Only then we will be in a position to follow step by step the evolution of our great civilisation.

ŚULIKA, CŪLIKA AND CŪLIKĀ-PAIŚĀCĪ.

Lacôte in his *Essai sur Guṇāḍhya* (p. 52) explains *Cūlikā-Paiśācī* as "low paiśācī" ("basse paiśācī"), and connects the word *Cūlikā* with Pali *culla*. According to him the name would be of the type *Ardhamāgadhī*. But it should be pointed out that one would expect here rather *cullikā* than *cūlikā*. *Culla*, derived from *kṣudra*, means "small, little" and does not offer a suitable explanation as the attribute of a dialect. Besides we have *Ardhamāgadhī* but not *Cūlikā-māgadhī*. Lacôte's explanation therefore does not seem to be satisfactory.

Lacôte has summarised (*loc. cit.*) all that is known about *Cūlikā-Paiśācī*. Hemchandra (according to whom it is *Cūlikā-Paiśācikā*) and Trivikrama mention it as a variety of Paiśācī. Mārkaṇḍeya Kavīndra speaks of three varieties of Paiśācī—Kaikeya, Śaurasena, and Pāñcāla. An unknown author mentions eight : Kāñci-deśīya, Pāṇḍya, Māgadha, Gauḍa, Vrācaḍa, Dākṣiṇātya, Śabara, and Drāviḍa. But the three mentioned by Mārkaṇḍeya are really Prakrits and the others are *deśabhāṣā*. A modern authority, Lakṣmīdhara, gives an original list of Paiśācīs, probably based on earlier sources : Pāṇḍya, Kekaya, Bāhlika, Sahya, Nepāla, Kuntala, and Gandhāra. Of these, those of the North-West, Kaikeya (the Western Punjab), Bāhlika (Balkh), Gandhāra (Peshawar) and Vrācaḍā (Sindh) might really have represented varieties of Paiśācī (*cf*. Grierson, *The Piśāca Languages of North-Western India*, p. 4.). It should be noted that all these names are of geographical import. We may, therefore, expect that *Cūlikā-Paiśācī* also had a similar significance.

Pargiter in 1912 (J. R. A. S., 1912, pp. 711-711, *Cūlikā Paiśācika Prakrit*) tried to connect it with a people called *Cūlika*, mentioned in the Sanskrit text. But he failed to prove the real existence of a people of that name. The Mahābhārata (VI, 75, 3297) mentions the Cūlikas along with the Tuṣāras, Yavanas and Śakas as occupying the right flank of the army in the great war. According to the Matsya Purāṇa[1] (50.76) the Cūlikas founded

1. This is according to the reading of the Calcutta and Ānandāśrama editions. Pargiter quotes the different forms from other MSS. too of which *Pulika*, *Calika*, *Valiṅka*, are simply misreadings and *Bāhlika* simply replaces a less known people by a better known one.

some sort of kingdom in India during the dark times of the Kali age. The Vāyu Purāṇa (99.268) has the same passage but reads *Tūlikas* instead.[2] "There can be little doubt from all these readings," says Pargiter, "that Cūlika is the best supported form of the name and many of the variations are easy misreadings or corruptions of it. Both the Purāṇas couple the Yavanas with them in this passage as having also founded a kingdom in India during that time.

"The Mārkaṇḍeya P. mentions the Culikas or Cūlikas along with the Lampākas, Kirātas, Kāśmiras, and other less known tribes in the region bordering India on the North (57.40) ; and the Cūlikas, along with the Aparāntikas, Haihayas, Pañcadakas (probably Pañcanadas), Tārakṣuras (probably Turuṣka) and other tribes who cannot be identified, in the very West of India (58.37). These Cūlikas are no doubt one and the same.

"The Matsya and the Vāyu Purāṇas have a passage corresponding to the former of these passages in the Mārkaṇḍeya, and the Vāyu has a further passage corresponding to Mārkaṇḍeya (57.41) which contains *Śūlikas* as another tribe in the same northern region. Corresponding to the Culikas of the Mārkaṇḍeya, the Vāyu reads *Pīḍikas*[3] (var. *Cūḍikas*) which the Matsya reads Sainikas (114.43). Culika and Cūḍika may be mere variations of the same name, as nearly as the geograpical compiler could get it, but whether that be so or not, the Vāyu reads (in all editions and MSS.) *Cūlika* instead of *Śūlika* in the second corresponding passage so that the Vāyu certainly places the Cūlikas as a tribe in the northern region."

The Brahma P. mentions in the corresponding passage *Śūlika* and the Brahmāṇḍa, the *Jhillika* (Kirfel, *Die Kosmographie der Inder*, p. 73). Therefore it seems that the same name appears under the following different forms : *culika, cūlika, cūḍika, śūlika, sūlika*, and *jhillika* (?) of which *cūlika* and *śūlika* are the most frequent. Both

2. Other MSS. give *culika, vulika, vunika* (*vutika*) and *vrulika*. See Pargiter (*loc. cit.*). The last forms are only misreadings. Confusion between *ca* and *va* is frequent in old texts. *Cf.* *cakṣu* for *vakṣu* (Oxus).

3. In the corresponding passage of the Vāyu Alberuni reads *Sulika* (Sachau, p. 300).

of them appear as the variants of the same name and both are located in the same region, either the North or the North-West.

The *Śūlikas* are known from other texts too which have been already discussed by Gauthiot (*J. As*, 1910, 11, pp. 541-542). The Śūlikas are mentioned like the Cūlikas, in the company of the Tukhāra, Yavana, Pahlava, Cīna, etc. According to the Matsya P. their country is watered by the river Cakṣu (Vakṣu, the Oxus),[1] The Vāyu P., as already seen, locates them in the North while the Bṛhatsaṁhitā places them in the North-West and mentions them six times (IX, 15, 21 ; X, 7 ; XIV, 23 ; XVI, 35 and XIV, 8, in the lastplace as *Śaulika*). Caraka(30.6) mentions them along with the Bāhlika, Pahlava, Cīna, Yavana and Śaka. In the *Fan-yu-tsa-ming* of Li-yen, a Sanskrit-Chinese vocabulary of the 7th-8th century A. D. and in a fragmentary lexicon of about the same period the name *Surī* (= *Sulī*) is given as an equivalent of *Hu*, "barbarians," applied by the Chinese only to the Sogdians in that period. They are mentioned in the company of the *Pārasī* (Pārasika), *Trusaka gaṇa* (Turuṣka°), *Karpiśaya* (Kapiśā), *Tukhāra*, *Kucīnaṁ* (Kucha), etc.[2] The Tibetan sources mention them as Sulik.

The identity of *Śūlika* and Sogdiana has been established by Gauthiot (*loc. cit.* and *Essai de Grammaire Sogdienne*, p. vi). The Chinese name of the country, *Su-li* falls back on an original : **Sūlīk* ∠ **Suwδik*, an eastern and southern dialectal form of Sogdian **Suγ-δik*. Pehlvi has *Surāk*, which is read as **Sūlik*. We have thus the following authentic forms of the same name (for the additional forms see Gauthiot, *loc. cit.*) :

Mahābhārata	:	*Cūlika.*
Purāṇas	:	*Culika, Cūlika, Cūḍika.*
		Śulika, Śūlika.
		Sulika (Alberuni).
Tibetan	:	*Śulik.*
Chinese	:	*Su-li* ∠ **Sūlīk* ∠ **Suγ-δik.*
Sino-Skt.	:	*Surī* ∠ *Sulī* ∠ *Sūli(k).*

1. In the corresponding passage quoted by Alberuni (Sachau, p. 261) the name is read as *Dhūlik* (?)

2. P. C. Bagchi, *Deux Léxiques Sanskrit-Chinois*, Paris, 1929, pp. 295 and 886.

Pehlvi	:	*Surāk*=*Sūlīk*	(agree with the eastern and southern dialectal forms of Sogdian).
Pehlvi (also)	:	*Soδ*	(agree with the northern and western dialectal forms of Sogdian).
Persian	:	*Suγd*	
Avesta		*Suγda*—.	
Greek	:	Σογδοι.	

How to explain the alternative forms *Culika-Śūlika* attested by the Purāṇas ? It seems that the name being that of a foreign people was heard and transcribed in Sanskrit in different ways. The alternance s : ś : c is not unknown in such cases. The name of Kucha is transcribed in the Bṛhat-saṁhitā as Kucīka of which a variant Kuśika is also recorded (Lévi, *J. As.*, 1913, p. 345) and it is quite possible, as has been suggested by Pargiter, that the name *Samarkand* appears in that of *Carmakhaṇḍika*, a country located by the Puranic sources in the northern region by the side of Pahlava, Yavana, Gandhāra (Kirfel, *loc. cit.*, p. 72 ; Alberuni, p. 300) Moreover the interchange between ś, *s* and *ch* is not unknown in the Middle Indo-Aryan even on Indian soil, *e. g.*, *chāva* ∠ skt. *śāba*. *chāvaa* ∠ skt. *śābaka* ; *chui*—skt. *śuciḥ* ; *chutā*—skt. *sudhā*. (Pischel *Prakrit Sprach.*, § 211). In Indo-Iranian such changes *ch*=*s*, *cy*=*s* were common ; *cf*. Sogdian *sy'kh (sayāka)*, Persian *sāya*, Sanskrit *chāyā* ; Sogd. *kyśp'* : *keśpa*—*kasyapa*, Skt. *kacchapa* (Gauthiot, *Grammaire Sogdienne*, §§ 162 & 118.). Therefore it seems evident that the Sogdian name *Sulik*, *Śulik* could be transcribed as *Śulika*-*Śūlika* and sometimes as *Culika*-*Cūlika*. The alternance recorded by the Purāṇas thus receives justification.

If the identity of *Cūlika-Śūlika* and Sogdian is thus taken as established then *Cūlikā-Paiśācī* may be considered to have been a variety of north-western Prakrit spoken by the Sogdians. Before proceeding to discuss the linguistic aspect of the problem it is necessary to see whether it was historically possible in any period of Indian history.

The Sogdians who are mentioned in Indian literature in the company of their neighbours the Tukhāras, the Pahlavas, the Yavanas, etc., appeared in India probably along with them. But though some of the Puranic texts attribute to them a certain political ascendancy in the history of India we have no other distinct proof in its support. Already in the first century B. C. the Śakas, and a little later the great *Yue-che* hordes, occupied the home of the Sogdians in the Oxus valley. They freely mixed with the people and borrowed their culture. There was, therefore, every possibility of Sogdians having come with these conquering hordes when they entered India.

The Sogdians were playing a great role in the history of Central Asia in this period. A large part of the trade between China and the Western countries was in their hands. The merchants of this country were so very enterprising that in the subsequent period they had small colonies in different parts of Eastern Turkestan up to the walls of China. Their language had become a sort of *lingua franca* in that region (See Pelliot, *Revue d'histoire et de Littérature religieuses*, 1911, p. 10ff.). Politically they did not seem to have played any great role even in their own country. But they were good agriculturists and excellent merchants. It is quite probable that in their latter capacity they had come up to India already towards the beginning of the Christian era. In the notice on China in the *Periplus of the Erythrean Sea* (Schoff, p. 48) we find that the commodities of China, specially cotton and silk stuffs, used to be brought by caravans in those days through Bactriana to Barygaza for exportation. This commerce was in all appearance partly in the hands of the Bactrians and their neighbours, the Sogdians. It is not improbable that these Sogdians had formed settlements in the Punjab by the side of the *Yue-ches* and *Śakas*. The biography of the Buddhist monk Seng-hui, preserved in the Chinese texts, clearly tells us that "he was born of a Sogdian family long established in India. His father was a merchant and went to Tonkin where he later settled down for his business. Seng-hui was born there" (Bagchi, *Le Canon Bouddhique en Chine*, I, p. 304.). Seng-hui went to China in 274 A. D. and was therefore born towards the beginning of the 3rd century A. D His family, consequently, had come to settle in India sometime in the 2nd century A. D., if not earlier. This case could not have been an isolated one. There were no doubt other families which had come up to India in the same period. Even in modern times we find groups of people in the Punjab who are most probably of foreign origin and bear names which may be connected either with *Śūlika-Cūlika* or with Suγ-δik—*Suγd*. First of all in the Shahpur district we meet with an agricultural clan of the Rajputs—known as the *Sulki* (*A Glossary of the Tribes and Castes of the Punjab*, 1919, Vol. III, p. 435). In Multan there are two classes of the Jāts, both agricultural, called *Solgi*, and *Solkah* (*ibid*, p. 428). Moreover there is another people in the Punjab, supposed to be of "mysterious origin", which is differently known as *Sud*, *Suda*, *Sudgi*. "The Suds are almost entirely confined to the lower hills and the districts that lie immediately under them as far west as Amritsar. Their headquarters are at Ludhiana, and the neighbouring town of Macchiwara and they are apparently unknown outside the Panjab. They are almost wholly mercantile in their pursuits......Many of them practise widow marriage" (*Ibid*, p. 430). They are mostly Hindu and only a few of them are Sikhs. But they are very lax in the observance of their respective religions. They freely take meat and wine. In the same notice it is further observed that "the tribe is apparently an ancient one but no definite information as to its origin is obtainable. They are proverbially acute and prosperous men of business." The Jārttikas (the ancient name of the modern Jāts) who lived about Śākala (Sialkot) were intimately connected with the Bāhikas, who are identified with the Bāhlikas. Their customs and manners are also denounced as un-Aryan in ancient texts. The characteristics of the people mentioned before and their low position in the Hindu society point out to their foreign origin. If they are connected with the ancient Sogdian immigrants then we have to suppose that the group *Sulki*, *Solgī*, *Solkah* was related to the Sūlikas—the Sogdians of the eastern and southern provinces of Sogdiana and the *Sud*, *Suda*, *Sudgi* were related to *Suγd*, or Suγ-δik, the Sogdians of the western and northern parts of the country. But it should be admitted that nothing can be definitely asserted until a closer study of these clans are made.

We might further note that there is a Rajput clan of the *Agnikula* who are connected with the Gujars (Gurjaras)—a Scythic people who probably followed the Huns to India. It is the *Cālukyas*. "Two branches of them migrated from Northern

India. One called *Cālukya*, descended from the Siwalik hills in the last quarter of the 6th century A. D., and penetrated into Southern India. The other, the Cālukya or *Solanki* left Kanauj about 950 A. D. and occupied Guzerat. *Solanki* Rajputs are still to be found in the Punjab in Hoshiarpur and in the tracts bordering on Rajputana in the South-West of the province (*Ibid*, I, p. 47).

The origin of the Cālukyas is unknown. The legendary origin of this dynasty is found in several places. Bilhaṇa, a court-poet of the later Cālukyas, in his *Vikramāṅkadeva-carita* gives a story according to which the progenitor of this dynasty was born from Indra's *culuka*, (the hand hollowed for receiving water) while he was receiving water from Brahmā (R. G. Bhandarkar, *History of Deccan*, p. 180). Another legend, recorded in a late inscription of the Cālukyas would have us believe that they were born from the *culka*, the water-pot of Hārīti-Pañcaśikha. It should be noted that the Sanskrit lexicons however give the form *caluka* and *culuka* instead of *culka* (*Cf*. Fleet, *Dynasties of the Kanarese Districts*, p. 339). All these seem to be legends arising out of popular etymologies suggested by the word *cālukya*. Cālukya however is not the only form of the name. Fleet (*loc. cit.*, p. 336, n. 3) has collected the other forms together. The oldest is *calkya* (578 A. D.), then come *calikya* (602 A. D.), *calikya, calukya* (634-35 A. D.), *caulukya* (757 A. D.), *calukki*, or *calukika*, and *cālukya*. All these forms seem to have evolved from *Calkya*. The *Çaulukya* or *Caulukika* dynasty of Anhilwaḍ was in all probability related to the Cālukyas. They are commonly known as *Solaki* or *Solanki* which is supposed to be a dialectic variant of Caulukya (*History of Gujrat*, Bombay Gazetteer, p. 156). All these different names seem to fall back on *Calkya* and **Solka*, which may be connected with *Śulki-Solgi-Solkah* of the Punjab and ultimately with *Cūlika-Śūlika*. It should be remembered that amongst the different forms of the last two names, already mentioned, we come across with *Calika*, and *Śaulika*.

Thus assuming that the Sogdians had come up to India along with the *Śaka-Yavana-Pahlava* about the Christian Era it is quite natural to expect that they had formed settlements of their own in the Punjab. In their intercourse with the Indians they probably had to adopt the Prakrit spoken in north-western India like their companions. The phonetic peculiarities of their own language were sure to influence the Prakrit adopted by them and ultimately the Prakrit as spoken by them might have been recorded by the grammarians as *Cūlikā-Paiśācī.* No geographical limit can be defined for this Sogdian Prakrit. It was probably current and understood everywhere from the Punjab up to the Valley of the Oxus.

I have elsewhere described the role of the Sogdians in the transmission of Buddhism to China (*cf.* Bagchi, *India and China,* Bulletin of the Greater India Society). Buddhists were received in their country already in the 1st century B. C., and it was from there that Buddhism and Buddhist texts were first introduced to China. From the 2nd century A. D., the Sogdian monks were taking part in the translation of Buddhist texts into Chinese. Buddhist texts were translated and transcribed into Sogdian. There are Chinese translations of original texts which bear Sogdian stamp. Huber (B. E. F. E. O., VI, Nos. 1-2), studied some Buddhist texts in Chinese translation which contain astrological terms. These terms were explained by Huber as Persian but they were later on found to be Sogdian (Müller, *Sitzungberichte*, Berlin Academy, 1909, p. 726 ; Gauthiot, *Grammaire*, p. xii). Theie is therefore ample evidence to prove that the Sogdians were in close touch with India and their monks knew some original language of the Buddhist texts either Sanskrit or the north-western Prakrit in which the Prakrit Dhammapada was written down. This Prakrit as we know from other sources was current in the entire region from the Punjab to Kroraina (Loulan). The Sogdian Prakrit or the *Cūlikā-Paiśācī* was in all probability a variety of this Prakrit. The characteristics of this Prakrit accord well with those of Paiśācī, while a study of the phonetic peculiarities of Sogdian show that the same Prakrit as spoken by the Sogdians-agreed with what we know about *Cūlikā-Paiśācī.* It is therefore necessary to discuss the Sogdian phonetic system and the Sanskritic words as pronounced by the Sogdians. For this purpose I would refer to the Sogdian version of the *Vessāntara jātaka*

(Gauthiot, *J. As.*, 1912, pp. 163 ff. and 430 ff.) and the Sogdian transcript of the *Nīlakaṇtha dhāraṇī* (Gauthiot, J. R. A. S., 1912, pp. 629 ff.).

In summarising the characteristics of *Cūlikā-Paiśācī* Lacôte (*loc. cit.*) writes : "In Paiśācī the hardening is limited to *d* whereas it is general in *Cūlikā-Paiśācī.* The latter is particularly denounced as the speech of the common people by Bhoja who puts Paiśācī in the mouth of important personages. According to Hemacandra in Culikā-Paiśācī the treatment of the sonant stops has an absolute uniformity. All of them undergo identical alteration *whatever their position in the word may be,* whether they are simple or aspirated, intervocalic or in a conjunct. This phenomenon is absolutely foreign to all Prakrits. It is reasonable to admit that it was produced in a non-Aryan population which did not posses the sonant stop in their original language." Grierson (*loc. cit.*) adds : "Hemacandra (IV, 327) states that according to some authorities *Cūlikā-Paiśācikā* does not harden soft consonants when they are initial or conjunct."

These characteristics agree well with those of Sogdian. Ancient Sogdian had only the surds *k, t, p* ; it had no sonants but only the spirants, γ, δ, β instead, It had also the occlusives *g, d, b* only after the nasals and in some rare consonant groups of ancient origin (Gauthiot, *Grammaire*, § 8). Therefore as we shall see later on Sogdian had generally used the surds for the sonant group in Skt. In initial positions and sometimes in conjunct the sonant group in Sanskrit has been replaced by the spirants.[1] There is only one difference to be taken into account, that though the Prakrit Grammarians speak of the existence of the aspirate in Culikā-P. there is no aspirate in Sogdian. "The aspirates of the Indian languages are always rendered in Sogdian by simple corresponding occlusives and the *h* represents in Sogdian writing not a consonant but a vowel : *lykh* should be read : **leka*" (Gauthiot, *A propos de la datation en Sogdien,* J. R. A. S., 1912, p. 333.)

1 It should however be noted that towards the beginning of the Christian era the Middle Indo-Aryan possessed the spirants which were later on dropped from the pronounciation. Thus Saurasenī of *circa* 200 A. D. had medially something like the following sounds : γ, δ, β, (v). It had also the double consonants. *Cf.* S. K. Chatterji, *Origin and Development of the Bengali Language*, p. 254.

But we cannot always implicitly rely on what the Prakrit Grammarians tell us about Cūlikā-P. It should be borne in mind that their knowledge of the language was only traditional and the examples supplied by them might have been greatly artificial. They might not have faithfully rendered the aspirate of the Indian languages as pronounced by the foreigners.

It remains to be noted that Sogdian did not possess either *ṭ, ṭh,* or *ḍ, ḍh* sounds but still in the transcription of the *dhāraṇī* it has always rendered *ḍ* of Sanskrit by *ṭ*. Before quoting the examples for better comparison we might give the following table of alternances :

Sanskrit	Cūlikā-P	Sogdam
g, gh	*k, kh* (?)	*k*
j, jh	*c, ch* (?)	*c,*
ḍ, ḍh	*ṭ, ṭh* (?)	*ṭ*
d, dh	*t, th* (?)	*t*
b, bh	*p, ph* (?)	*p*
v	p	*β*(= bilabial *v*)

Sanskrit	Cūlikā-P	Sogdian
g gh	*k kh*	
giritataṭam	*kiritaṭam*	*kut'ykh* ∠ *ghaṇṭikā*
gharmaḥ	*khammo*	*nyak'tn* = *nirghātana*
nagaran	*nakaram*	*sβkws* ∠ *Śivaghoṣa*
meghaḥ	*mekho*	
j jh	*c ch*	
jīmūtaḥ	*cīmūto*	*c'r'ynh* ∠ *jalin*
jharjharaḥ	*chaccharo*	*cyn'y* ∠ *jināya*
rājā	*rācā*	*c'ycy* ∠ *jīji*
nirjharaḥ	*niccharo*	*r'cβwrt* ∠ *rājyavardhana*
		βacr ∠ *vajra*
		nyr'cwt'' ∠ *nirjjautā*
ḍ ḍh	*ṭ th*	
ḍamarukaḥ	*ṭamaruko*	*tr'wm* ∠ *ḍrum*
ḍhakkā	*ṭhakkā*	

Sanskrit	Cūlikā-P	Sogdian
taḍāgam	*taṭākam*	
maṇḍalam	*maṁtalam*	*munṭ ṭ'ṭ'* ∠ *muṇḍaṭaṭe*
gāḍham	*kāṭham*	*ngr knṭ* ∠ *Nilakaṇṭha*
d dh	*t th*	
Dāmodaraḥ	*Tāmotaro*	*muır'y* ∠ *mandrī*
dhūli	*thūlī*	*tutr'k* ∠ *Dandarak*
Sadanam	*Satanam*	*wyspyδr'k* ∠ *Vessāntara*
pradeśaḥ	*pateso*	*''n'nt* ∠ *Ananda*
Vadanakam	*vatanakam*	
Kandarpaḥ	*Kamtappo*	*pwty'st* } ∠ *Buddha°*
madhuram	*mathuram*	*pwty'kh* }
		pwty }
		pwt'y ∠ *bodhaya*
		śat'wδn ∠ *Śuddhodana*
		yśwδrh ∠ *Yaśodhārā*
		t'rny ∠ *dhāraṇī*
		syt'y ∠ *siddhāya*
b bh	*p ph*	
bālakaḥ	*pālako*	*prm'nh* ∠ *Brāhmaṇa*
bhagavatī	*phakavatī*	*pwt'y* ∠ *bodhaya*
rabhasaḥ	*raphaso*	
ḍimbam	*ṭimpam*	
v	*p*	*β*
vanam	*palam*	*βacr* ∠ *vajra*
Govindaḥ	*Gopinto*	*nyrβ'n* ∠ *nirvāṇa*
		βr'ysmn ∠ *Vaiśramaṇa*
		sβkwś ∠ *śivaghoṣa*

III

KUCHEAN OR WESTERN ARSI

A forgotten language of the Indo-European family.

Prof. Sylvain Lévi has just published a work called the *Fragments de Textes Koutchéens.* This book contains the fragments of the ancient Kuchean translations of four Buddhist texts, viz. the *Udānavarga, Udānastotra, Udānālaṁkāra* and *Karmavibhaṅga.* Some of these fragments belong to the collection of the Pelliot Mission, some to the Stein and a few others to the Russian Mission. An earlier British collection of manuscripts from Central Asia, placed at the disposal of Hoernle also contained some Kuchean manuscripts and these also were sent to M. Lévi for decipherment and interpretation.

The present work contains the Kuchean texts, their French translation, a vocabulary with references to the forms of words in a cognate dialect called "Tokharian A," comparative notes and an Introductory Essay in which various problems relating to the language and the country in which it was spoken have been treated.

The texts written in the Kuchean language which were previously published contained the fragment of some medical treatises originally translated from a text similar to Caraka and Suśruta. The fragments belonging to the Weber and Macartney collection were edited and published by Hoernle in the *Journal of the Asiatic Society of Bengal*, 1901 (Extra number I, Appendix) but for want of necessary materials Hoernle was unable to interpret it. M. Lévi studied some fragments of a similar treatise belonging to the Pelliot collection and these fragments are all bilingual containing the Sanskrit text by the side of its Kuchean translation

Besides these medical treatises and some passports noticed by M. Lévi all the literary remains of ancient Kuchean so far published are fragments of Buddhist texts. M. Lévi previously published some bilingual portions of *Dharmapada* and a Kuchean translation of the Vinaya of the Sarvāstivāda school.

Udānavarga has been edited from Kuchean mss. coming from

different collections namely of Pelliot, Stein, Hoernle (Weber-Macartney) and Berezowski. The Sanskrit *Udānavarga* for a long time known only from its Chinese and Tibetan translations are now available from publications of Lévi, de La Vallée Poussin, Pischel and N. P. Chakravarti relating to Sanskrit mss. discovered by various Archaeological Missions in Central Asia. The Kuchean fragments contain translations from most of the Vargas of the *Udānavarga* I-II, IV, VIII-IX, X, XII, XVI, XVII-XVIII, XIX-XX, XXII, XXIII, XXVIII, XXIX, XXXI, XXXII XXXIII, and they show that a complete translation of the text once existed in Kuchean. The variety of mss. also proves that the text was widely read in the monasteries of Kucha.

The other two texts *Udānastotra* and *Udanālaṁkāra* are as yet unknown in their original. The former is a collection of verses eulogising each of the *Vargas* of the *Udānavarga* and the latter is a sort of versified commentary of the *Udānavarga* which explains the verses and also relates the circumstances under which a particular verse of the text had been pronounced by Buddha. Both these texts are not bilingual and in the present state of our knowledge it is difficult to say if they were translated from Sanskrit or were originally composed in Kuchean.

The 4th text has been called by Lévi *Un Poème en Koutchéen sur la Retribution des Actes* (*Karmavibhaṅga*). It consists of a few fragments in the Pelliot collection of a Kuchean text which has been proved to be the metrical paraphrase of a Sanskrit Buddhist text called the *Karmavibhaṅga*. The ms. of this Sanskrit text was discovered by M. Lévi from Nepal in 1922. It has now been edited and published by him in a work in which he has given all the parallel texts from Pali, Tibetan, Chinese and Kuchean, as well as illustrations from plastic representations of some of the stories of the text in the bas-reliefs of the famous temple of Borobodour in Java. In this work M. Lévi has studied the text in its various aspects and has brought out the importance of the text in the Buddhism of different countries.

One of the most important archaeological discoveries of the 20th century is no doubt Kuchean, an independent language of the Indo-European family which had long fallen into oblivion. The explorations undertaken by the different missions, the Russian, British, French, German as well as the Japanese in different parts of Central Asia brought to light fragments of ancient manuscripts and writings of other description and it is from them that some scholars in France and Germany discovered the two dialects of an Indo-European language long forgotten but once spoken in the northern parts of Eastern Turkestan, in the region of Kucha and Karasahr. Of the two dialects which have been so long marked A and B the first has been deciphered and interpreted from the mss. of the German collection of Grünwedel and Von Lecoq by Messrs Sieg and Siegling. The second dialect has been deciphered and interpreted by M. Lévi from the French collection of mss. made by the Pelliot Mission. Other mss. written in this dialect and belonging to the collection made by the British, Japanese and Russian missions were also placed at the disposal of M. Lévi. The documents written in the A dialect came from the region of Karasahr and its neighbourhood whereas those in the B dialect were discovered in the region of Kucha and its adjoining places.

Scholars have not been as yet unanimous in naming this language. While M. Lévi cautiously suggested that the A dialect should be called Karasahrian and the B dialect Kuchean, Messrs Sieg and Siegling preferred to call them Tokharian A and B and maintain that they represent the two dialects of the forgotten language spoken by the Yue-ches or the Indo-Scythians. Their only evidence was the colophon of an Uigur text called *Maitrisimit* (Skt. Maitreyasamiti). The colophon which is in the Uigur language says that the work was originally translated from the Indian text into Toxri and from Toxri into Turkish (*anətkak tīlīntin toxri tīlīnca yarətmiś...toxri tīlīntin türk aqtarmiś*). As a translation of the *Maitreya-samiti* in the A dialect had been discovered by the German Mission it was maintained that this latter was the basis of the Turkish translation and that the A dialect is no other than the Toxri or Tokharian mentioned in the colophon of the Uigur text. Such an argument cannot be deemed conclusive, particularly in matters of the antiquities of Central Asia which was the meeting place of a large number of people and languages in ancient times. It is thus quite conceivable that the translations of the Skt. *Maitreyasamiti* existed also in languages other then the A dialect and that Toxri had nothing to do with it.

M. Lévi has again discussed the problem in his present book and shown that in the present state of our knowledge we cannot establish any connection between the two dialects and ancient Tokharian. The Tokharians lived in a country far away from the region of Kucha and Karasahr. Their country called by the Chinese *Tu-ho-lo* (Skt. Tukhāra) is located according to the Chinese evidence in the Upper Valley of the Oxus between the Hindukush on the South and the Oxus on the North whereas the Pamirs formed its eastern boundary. Besides the name of the people in all its ancient forms—Skt. Tukhāra, Gk. Tokharoi, Chinese *Tu ho-lo*—is pronounced with a strong aspirate while there is no aspirate in any of the two dialects A and B.

None of the two dialects again has any connection with the Indo-Scythians or the Yue-ches. The earliest Chinese evidences about this people tell us that in the middle of the 2nd century B. C. their hordes being defeated at the hands of the Hiung-nus retired to the West and settled down in the valley of the Oxus where Chang-kien met them in 128 B. C. Those who were left behind and took shelter amongst the barbarians living along the southern steppes of Eastern Turkestan came to be known as the Little Yue-ches. According to the *Wei Lio* which deals with the history prior to the middle of the 3rd century A. D. the Great Yue-ches, settled in the valley of the Oxus, gradually extended their suzerainty on the kingdoms of *Ki-pin* (Kashmir), *Ta-hia* (Bactriana), *Kao-fu* (Kabul) and *T'ien-chu* (India). Kumārajīva who lived towards the end of the 4th and beginning of the 5th century A. D. identifies the Little Yue-ches with the Tukhāras. The country which they occupied is located by some of the Chinese sources in the Pamirs. In short, none of the two divisions of the Yue-ches or the Indo-Scythians can be said to have settled in the northern region of Eastern Turkestan in which Kucha and Karasahr are situated. It is therefore risky to try to connect the two dialects with the Indo-Scythians in the present state of our knowledge.

On the other hand, there is ample evidence to show that the two dialects were known to the outsiders as the languages of the localities in which they were spoken, namely Kucha and Karasahr. M. Lévi in an earlier article (*Le Tokharien B, Langue de Koutcha*, *JAs.*, 1913, pp. 311-380) brought out in details the important role of Kucha in the ancient history of Eastern Turkestan and in the transmission of Buddhist civilisation to China. The Chinese sources record the important events of the history of this country from the middle of the 2nd century B. C. to the 11th century A. D. During this long period of her history Kucha often appears as the unquestionable mistress of the countries along the northern route of Eastern Turkestan ; she often appears fighting with the invading Chinese forces for her independence. When defeated she appears as an ally of China but to re-assert her independence at the earliest opportune moment. Kucha was converted to Buddhism at an early period and for a long time the Buddhist scholars of the country played an important part in the transmission of Buddhism to China. Some of them were instrumental in translating Buddhist texts into Chinese and amongst them the name of Kumārajīva remains immortal. It is again a monk of Kucha named Li-yen who seems to have been one of the oldest authors of a Sanskrit-Chinese lexicon for the use of the Chinese Buddhist scholars. In some cases the Chinese translations clearly seem to have been made from the Buddhist texts of which the originals were in the '*language of Kucha*'. M. Lévi has shown that some of the early transcriptions of Buddhist terms in Chinese were made from the Kuchean words, e. g., Sha-men—Kuch. *ṣamāne* (Skt. śramana), sha-mi—Kuch. *ṣanmir* (Skt. śramaṇera), po-ye-t'i—Kuch. *pāyti* (Skt. pāyantika), etc. In the account of the travels of Wu-k'ong written in 787 A. D. four independent languages of the "*Four Chinese Garrisons of Central Asia*" are recognised and these are the languages of *Kucha*, *Karasahr*, *Kasghar* and *Khotan*.

The role of Karasahr so far as it can be gathered from the Chinese records is comparatively less important than that of Kucha. In the present work M. Lévi has collected all the available information on Karasahr and Turfan, the country in its neighbourhood.

These two countries comprised the area in which the A dialect seems to have been spoken because most of the documents written in the A dialect have been discovered from this area. Karasahr in the Chinese records is mentioned as Yen-k'i and under its allied forms and in the records of Hiuan-tsang as *A-k'i-ni.* The original of this name has now been discovered from the Central Asian record by Prof. Lüders. The country in some of these documents is clearly mentioned as *Agnideśa.* Turfan occurs in the Chinese annals under the name Kao-ch'ang. The role of these two countries in the political history of Eastern Turkestan as well as in the transmission of Buddhist civilisation to China is less significant when compared to that of Kucha.

Prof. Lüders has discovered the names of some kings of Karasahr from the Central Asian records. These names end in the word *Arjuna* e.g. Indrārjuna, Candrārjuna etc. On the other hand in the Chinese records 'Po' which means 'white' is a regular title of the kings of Kucha. As Arjuna also means 'white' in Sanskrit it has been suggested that 'Po' is nothing but a Chinese translation of the title Arjuna. Arjuna in the B dialect occurs under the form *Arcuni* (e.g. Kṣemārcune).

Under these circumstances it is possible to conceive that the two countries Kucha and Karasahr played quite distinct roles in the history of Eastern Turkestan and there is every justification in considering the two dialects as local languages of the two countries Kucha and Karasahr.

But is it possible to find a common name which may comprise the two dialects, A and B ? In some of the documents written in the A. dialect there is reference to an Ārśi speeeh—e. g. *ārśi kantu, ārśi nu kantwā, ārśi-niṣkramā(ntaṁ), ārśi-lāñcinaṁ* etc. The grammatical construction of some of these passages shows that the word *ārśi* was treated as a foreign word, because it appears without an inflexion which is contrary to the spirit of the language. M. Lévi has shown that Ārśi represents a local pronunciation of Chinese *An-si* (lit. Pacified West), a name given to this region in the middle of the 7th century A. D. when the country was annexed to China. Though this is a late name, M. Lévi has suggested that for the sake of convenience it may be used as the common name of the two dialects and the A dialect spoken in the region of Karasahr may be distinguished as *Eastern Ārśi* and the dialect spoken in the region of Kucha as *Western Ārśi*.

These two languages have appeared to be dialects of an Indo-European language hitherto unknown. This language has been considered to be a western dialect of Indo-European because the Indo-European prepalatals are represented in it by *k* as in Latin *centum* e. g. in dialect B. *kante* (the word for 100), *okdh* (the word for 8). *naksentr* (cf. Tkt. naśyati), etc. But Prof. Meillet in his "Linguistic Remarks" on this language has uttered a word of caution by saying that this simple fact that the prepalatals are represented in the Ārśi languages by *k* is not sufficient to authorise us in grouping it with the *centum* languages. The eastern dialects of Indo-European namely the Indo-Iranian, Slavonic, Baltic, Albanian and Armenian, as far as these consonants are concerned, do not represent the state of any common period of these dialects. The Sanskrit forms with *j* and Armenian with *c* show clearly that the language had at last arrived at the mid-occlusive stage and it appears to be most probable that in the common state of the eastern speeches the prepalatal pronunciation was a little palatalised : *k´ g´* etc. A regression of *k´* towards *k* was therefore possible. As far as the gutturals are concerned if we want to prove that Kuchean belonged to the Western group of Indo-European languages it will be necessary to show from it the labiovelar element of the Latin series *quid*. But its trace is not very clear in Kuchean. Under these circumstances it is safer to consider the two dialects of the Ārśi speech as an Indo-European language quite independent of all hitherto known languages of that family. In this language the greatest confusion of the consonants takes place. The four kinds of Indo-European occlusives—surds, aspirated surds, sonants and aspirated sonants are reduced to only *p, t, k*. The two kinds of guttural occlusives—the prepalatal and velar—can be distinguished only in a few cases and with great difficulty. The palatal c is only a form of dental *t* before prepalatal vowels and before *v*. There are however two series of occlusives in this anguage—*p, t, k*, and p, dh (rather t because it is also a surd) and k but the distinction between these two series depends on facts of pronunciation resulting from the internal development of the language and has no etymological value which can be now clearly ascertained.

It is more difficult to determine the vowel changes in this language because in matters of vowel changes in Indo-European the starting points are often uncertain. M. Meillet records the following changes in the Ārśi languages : *e* strongly yodised has either become (*y*)*a* whence *a* or (*y*)*e* whence *io, o,* but *e* also represents the ancient *e* ; *o* has become *e.* As the alphabet was borrowed from India, in the writing the Ārśi languages distinguish between long and short but from the transcriptions of Sanskrit words in these languages it becomes evident that the notation does not represent the diffierence in quantity. The short and long in the writing do not correspond to the short and long of Sanskrit.

From a study of the transcription of Sanskrit words in Kuchean it has been also clearly ascertained that Kuchean did not possess any sonant stops except nasals, it did not possess any aspirates and its vowels were distinguished by quality. Some examples will make it clear :

Consonant changes—

i. *k<g, akaru* from Skt. *agaru, aśvakānta-aśvagandhā takaru—tugaru*

ii. *c<j : pṛṅkarac-bhṛṅgarāja, cagala-jagala, Cinasena-Jinasena*

iii. *t<d, Saṅkatasa-Saṅghudāsa, tinar-dīnāra, tanapate-dānapati*

t<ḍ, pitari-viḍārī

nt<ṇḍ, prapuntarik-prapuṇḍarīka

nt<nd, kuntark-gundraka

iv. *p<b, prohati—bṛhatī*
mp<mb, nicitakampa-nīcakadamba
p<v, punarṇapa-punarnavā, śāripa-śārivā

Loss of aspiration—

t<dh, veteni-vedhini, Putamitre-Buddhamitra
t<dh, matu—madhu, saintava-saindhava
t<t, musta-mustā
t<d, meta medā
t<ṭh, pāta-pāṭhā

Note :—About the indentification of the A. Dialect (Tokharian A) the view expressed here by Lévi has been modified in this book (supra, p. 28) in the light of later researches.

ABBREVIATIONS

BEFEO—	Bulletin de l'Ecole Française d'Extreme-Orient.
BSOS—	Bulletin of the School of Oriental and African Studies, London.
J. As.—	Journal Asiatique.
JRAS—	Journal of the Royal Asiatic Society.
MSL—	Mémoire, Société Linguistique de Paris.

BIBLIOGRAPHY

Bagchi P. C.— Le Canon Bouddhique en Chine. 2 vols.

— Deux Lexiques Sanskrit-Chinois. 2 vols.

— India and China.

Barua & Mitra— Kharosthi Dhammapada (Cal. Univ.).

Bailey H. W.— Khotanese Texts vol I.

— Hvatanica BSOS VIII, IX, X.

— Rama, Ibid X

— Indo-Turcica, Ibid IX

— Ttaugara, Ibid VIII

Beneveniste E.— Notes Sogdiennes BSOS IX

Boyer, Rapson & Sénart— Kharosthi Inscriptions discovered by Sir Aurel Stein in Chinese Turkestan, Text and translation.

Chakravarti N. P.— India and Central Asia

— L'Udānavarga Sanskrit

Chavannes E— Les Tou-kiues Occidentaux 1908

Filliozat J.— Fragment de Textes Koutchéens de Medicine et de Magie 1948.

Finot L— Prātimokṣa des Sarvāstivādins J. As. 1913

Gauthiot R.— De l'Alphabet Sogdien J. As. 1911

— Noms de nombre en Sogdien MSL 1911-12

— Une Version Sogdienne du Vessāntara Jātaka J. As. 1912.

— Essai de grammaire Sogdienne vol I 1914 ; vol II ; completed by E. Beneveniste 1928.

— Le Sūtra des causes et des effects de Bien et du Mal, 2 vols

— Nīlakaṇtha-dhāraṇī JRAS 1912

Grierson G.— Etymologies Tokhariennes *J As.*, 1912 pp. 339-44 ; [In this article Sir G. Grierson has compared some of the Kuchean words with words of the so-called Paiśācī group of languages].

Grousset R.— L'Empire des Steppes 1952

Henning W. B.— Argi and the Tokharians BSOS VIII

Hoernle R.— Manuscript Remains of Eastern Turkestan 1914

Hackin J.— Formulaire Sanskrit-Tibétain 1924

Lévi S.— Etude des Documents Tokhariens de la Mission Pelliot by S. Lévi with "Remarques Linguistiques" by A. Meillet—*J As.*, 1911, pp. 431-464.

— Etude des Documents Tokhariens de la Mission Pelliot by Lévi with "Remarques Linguistiques" by A. Meillet—*J As.*, 1911, pp. 119-150.

— Un fragment Tokharien du Vinaya des Sarvāstivadins (Hoernle Collection) by S. Lévi—*J As.*, 1912, pp. 101-116.

— Le "Tokharien B, la Langue de Koutcha"- by S. Lévi-*J As.*, 1913, pp. 311-380.

— Les noms qe nombre en Tokharien B by A. Meillet, *MSL.*, XLVII, pp. 281-294.

— Remarques sur les formes grammaticales de quelques textes en Tokharien B. (formes verbales) by Lévi and A. Meillet *MSL.*, XVIII.

— Remarques sur les formes grammaticales ......(formes nominales) by S. Lévi and A. Meillet, *MSL.*, XVIII, pp. 381-423.

— Les Nouvelles Langues Indo-Européenes trouvées en Asie Centrale—by A. Meillet, Revue de Mois 1912, XIV, p. 20., [*BEFEO.*, XII, 148].

— Tokharian Prātimokṣa Fragment by S. Lévi, *JRAS.*, 1913, p. 109.

— Kuchean Fragments (of Prātimokṣa Prāyaścittika and Pratideśanīya) by S. Lévi—in *Manuscript Remains from Eastern Turkestan*, ed by Hoernle, pp. 357 ff.

— Mahā-karmavibhaṅga et Karmavibhaṅgopadeśa (with the Kuchean text by S. Lévi, Paris 1932.

— Fragments de Text Koutchéens, S. Lévi—*Cahiers de la Société Asiatique* 1933.

— Textes Sanscrits de Touen-houang J. As. 1910.

— L'Apramādavarga J. As. 1912.

— Dṛṣṭāntapaṅkti et son auteur J. As. 1927.

— Manuscrits Sanscrits provénants de Bamiyan. J. As. 1932.

— Quelques documents sur le Bouddhisme Indien dans l'Asie Centrale BEFEO 1905.

Lüders H.— Des Śāriputraprakaraṇa ein drama des Aśvaghoṣa, 1911

— Brüchstüke des Kalpanāmaṇḍitikā des Kumāralāta 1926

— Zur Geschichte und Geographie Ostturkestans, 1922

— Uber die litterarischen Funden in Ost-Turkestan 1912

Pelliot Paul— — Mission en Asie Centrale (Bull. de la Soc. de Geogr., 1908)

— Rapport de M. Pelliot sur sa Mission, 1910

— Trois ans dans la Haute-Asie (Asie Franc. 1910

— Une bibliothéque médievale retrouvée au Kansou (*BEFFO*, 1908)

— Documents de la Mission Pelliot (Bull. arch. du Musee Guimet 1921)

— Une bilingue sogdien-chinoise (Melanges offerts a S. Lévi)-1911

— Influences iraniennes an Asie centrale Rev. Hist. Litt. Releg., 1912)

— Indian influences in the early Chinese Art in Tun-huang (Indian Art and letters 1926)

— Un fragment du Suvarṇaprabhāsasūtra en iranien-oriental (Mem. Soc. Ling. 1913)

— Le Cha tcheou etc. (J. As. 1916)

— Notes sur les anciens noms de Kuca, d'Aqsu et d'Uchturfan (T'oung Pao). 1923

— Les Grottes de Touen-houang, 6 vols (Plates) 1920-1924 —

— A propos du "tokharien" T'oung Pao XXXII.

— Tokharian et Koutchéen J. As. 1934.

— La Version ouigoure de l'histoire des prince Kalyāṇaṁkara et Pāpaṁkara, T'oung Pao 1914

Sieg and Siegling— Tocharische Sprachreste 1921

Stein, Sir Aurel— Ancient Khotan

— Serindia 3 vols

— Innermost Asia
(Geographical Journal) 1925

Thomas F. W. — Tibetan Literary Texts and Documents vols. I & II.

Waldschmidt E— Bruchstüke des Bhikṣuṇi-rātimokṣa der Sarvāstivādin 1926.

— Das Mahāparinirvāṇasūtra.

Watters— On Yuan Chwang 2 vols.

Woolner— Sanskrit names of Drugs in Kuchean by *JRAS.*, 1925, pp. 623 ff.

INDEX

CORRECTIONS

Page	*Incorrect*	*Correct*
1, 11	Ienessi	Ienessei
29, 6	tne	the
61, 3 (from bottom)	Cep	cap
63, 15	Tu-ho-co	Tu-ho-lo
21	Tsiu-umo	Tsiu-mo
39, 2 (from bottom)	Cche Kien	Che K'ien
64, 6 (from bottom)	Ke Lolaina	like...
66 last line	Raytiraya	Rayatiraya
76, 15	Ku Kuang	Lu Kuang
81, 16	this state	a state
89, 17	Buddhas of...	Buddhas or
97, 24	W-ti-ti-si-yu	Wu-ti...
98, 16	entilted	entitled
103, 25	Mātṛecta	Mātṛceṭa
104, 5	गत	गतः